DISCLAIMER:

This book does not provide financial advice and you should not treat any of the content as such. I do not recommend any cryptocurrency be bought, held, sold, or otherwise speculated on by you. You are solely responsible for conducting your own due diligence and consulting a financial advisor before making your own trading or investment decisions. Trading cryptocurrencies is a high-risk activity, which can result in significant financial losses. Under no circumstances will I be liable for any loss, damages (special, incidental, consequential, or any other type), or other negative consequences of any kind you or anyone else suffers as a result of any trading, speculating, or investing based on any information you receive through this book. All information highlighted in this book is for educational purposes only and does not assert or guarantee any future asset value or performance whatsoever. No warranties, express or implied, are given and are expressly waived. No assertions or guarantees are made as to the accuracy or completeness of this book and its contents.

All market participants should check with their regulators and relevant authorities to ensure their own compliance within the jurisdiction they reside or are a citizen thereof. This book does not assert the legality of anyone as a market participant nor does it assert that any actor in the space, whether an exchange or any other business or business affiliate, is compliant with any regulator or legal authority whatsoever. I make no claims or judgments as to the safety or soundness of any exchange, founding team, technology or supporting technology, or any other products or actors relevant to the industry. This book makes no legal judgments about anything, and market participants are strongly advised to seek legal advice from a professional before engaging in trading or otherwise speculating on cryptocurrencies.

Readers understand the performance statistics come from a limited sample size within the top 100 cryptocurrencies. All statistics are for educational use only, and readers should take into account any and all possible limitations of the study, which include, but are not limited to, small sample sizes, limited historical record, a latitude of subjectivity, and human error.

CONTENTS

II. TECHNICAL ANALYSIS   31

III. TRADE STRATEGIES AND THEORY   139

INTRODUCTION

The Chart Logic handbook is designed to give new traders all of the information they need to begin trading the cryptocurrency markets and offers experienced traders an easy go-to refresher with exclusive insights, statistics, and tactics. The goal of the handbook is to achieve profitable fluency in trading and to provide all traders and investors with the tools necessary to outperform a simple buy and hold investor. To this end, numerous resources exist but they neglect to offer an easy, quality, step-by-step guide. Chart Logic takes a complete beginner through all procedural steps necessary to use, buy, and sell cryptocurrencies. But the analyses, techniques, and strategies taught are designed to be useful both to novice traders and those with experience. The technical analysis and examples are based on traditional methods but are also uniquely tailored, crypto-centric, and come from five years of successfully trading cryptocurrencies. Furthermore, Chart Logic offers the first chart pattern performance statistics specific to the cryptocurrency markets (both for Bitcoin and USD-traded pairs), and the handbook is peppered with data-driven insights and analysis. Finally, traders will also learn comprehensive trade strategies and theory, including how to apply an evidence-based approach to tackling each trade.

For new traders, terminology is defined naturally as the handbook progresses, however, you may also skip to the Definitions Key in the back if you do not understand a word I am using. I try to introduce things quickly as they become relevant. If you are familiar with trading, using exchanges and wallets, and are uninterested in procedural steps, I suggest you skip to Part II of the handbook and continue with the technical and strategic sections.

Importantly, successful trading can vary drastically between different people. Successful trading is also not something that can be learned over night and often takes years of trial and error before a trader feels truly comfortable with their trading style and technique. The trading techniques I teach in this handbook are not mutually exclusive and only focus on a fraction of the full spectrum of technical analysis. I've found over the years that a simple trading strategy is a very effective strategy. I focus more on mastering core concepts rather than trying every widget and indicator under the sun. Indeed, many seasoned traders can tell you an overly complicated trade strategy is not often useful and may show inexperience. But this should not discourage you from experimenting with techniques not highlighted in this handbook, and it's not to say these methods are the only way speculators successfully trade a market. Each trader must find for themselves what works and what doesn't.

Part I of the handbook will briefly familiarize you with some of the core concepts of cryptocurrencies and leads a new user through wallets, exchanges, and trade procedure. Part II is dedicated to learning technical analysis from the perspective of never having seen a technical chart before to becoming fluent enough to trade. All examples for the technical analysis section are carefully cherry-picked from the cryptocurrency markets and are catered toward crypto-centric trading. Many reflect actual successful trades. The chart pattern analysis section offers performance-based statistics on all commonly occurring continuation and reversal patterns in the top 100 cryptocurrencies. Nearly 400 charts and more than 1,800 patterns were examined and tediously cataloged for this study. Feel free to examine all of them at chartlogic.io. Part III discusses trade strategies and theory, which covers proper risk management, introduces my evidence-based trade approach, discusses trading different market conditions and different types of cryptocurrencies, and offers various insights and considerations I wish a trader had taught me when I first started trading. Together, the procedure, technical analysis skill building, and essential trade strategies create the holy trinity necessary to trade cryptocurrency markets with confidence and discipline. Let's get started!

I. PRELIMINARIES AND TRADE PROCEDURE

CHAPTER 1:
PRELIMINARIES

Blockchain and Cryptocurrency – What Is It?

In layman's terms, a blockchain is a data ledger that uses a network of computers to create, verify, and secure transactions. Digital containers filled with transactions ("blocks") are linked together to form easily verifiable and secure transactional ledgers. Key properties of blockchains are their immutability, security, and decentralization.

Blockchains are constructed under two dominant consensus algorithms: Proof of Work (POW) and Proof of Stake (POS). Both systems share similarities with the key difference being who creates blocks of transactions and how. Under POW, computers called "miners" take bundles of unconfirmed transactions and compete to solve difficult equations required to discover a new block to contain them. When a miner successfully completes an equation, it's rewarded and forms the next block of validated transactions. Completed blocks are broadcast to a greater network of node computers that verify the validity of the transactions and the block's conformance to the rules of the network. Completed and verified blocks are strung together, creating an irreversible digital chain. Under POS, rather than using the heavy computational work of miners to create blocks of transactions, validator computers ("stakers") are randomly or semi-randomly chosen and rewarded for forging blocks based on collateral they stake to the network in the blockchain's native currency. Dishonest validators are punished and can be compelled to relinquish their stakes.

Cryptocurrencies (cryptos) are digital assets issued on a blockchain that are used for transactions such as payment and fees, and also for rewarding and incentivizing network participants. Users can send cryptos to each other like digital money, and cryptos are often used as a reward system to incentivize those who mine or stake to create and validate the blocks of transactions. In other words, cryptos are both a payment system for anybody wishing to use the software and a payment reward for the participants supporting the network with computing power.

Numerous types of blockchains and blockchain mechanics exist. These definitions barely scrape the surface of the complicated technology and are merely a simple introduction. I suggest interested readers take the time to educate themselves about the wonders of blockchain technology. However, for the purpose of this handbook, we are interested in the speculative aspect. We are in it for the money, not the tech. So, the introduction is brief.

Speculation

In addition to being used as a means of payment and reward, cryptos are traded on exchanges like a commodity or stock. Conceptually, as cryptos become more widely used and adopted, their value rises or falls based on user demand, scarcity of the asset, and in some cases cost of production. For example, Bitcoin will only ever have twenty-one million coins and nearly all of them have already been mined and put into global circulation. Mining today takes an enormous amount of electricity and it's costly to produce even a single bitcoin. Moreover, as more people buy, HODL, send, and spend Bitcoin, the less there is to go around. Thus, the price fluctuates over time because of use, scarcity, and production.

Today, thousands of cryptos exist serving scores of different purposes. Many are run by start-up companies, which held token sales called Initial Coin Offerings (ICOs) to fundraise their inception. These thousands of cryptos are offered to speculators on various exchanges where the public can buy, sell, and otherwise speculate on the future value of the digital assets. Importantly, traditional market analysis techniques like technical analysis may be applied to the crypto markets to aid speculators in their quest for fortune. This is the focus of the Chart Logic handbook.

Learn to Trade – Don't Just Be a HODLer

A driving purpose of this handbook is to outperform the average holder or "HODLer." A HODLer, by original description, was an investor who self-admitted he could not trade well. Today, the term is popularly used to define anyone who is holding cryptocurrency for the long haul. In other words, a long-term cryptocurrency investor. The famous term comes from a 2013 Bitcoin forum post where a Bitcoin trader goes off on a tirade about his inability to effectively call the highs and lows of price action, which presumably resulted in a loss of bitcoins in his stack. In the flurry of his emotional rant, the Bitcoin holder drunkenly writes that he is just going to "HODL" his Bitcoin for the long term rather than trade it. HODL became an iconic typo for the word HOLD and is commonly used today by crypto enthusiasts.

A HODLer enters the market, sometimes strategically or sometimes arbitrarily, but generally they intend to hold for many years under the theory that cryptos will increase in value over time regardless of the slumps and swings. The HODLer philosophy is not necessarily wrong. So long as cryptos continue to exist, some of the most useful and enduring assets will likely continue to appreciate due to use, supply, and demand. Historically, successful and enduring markets are on one long bull run with intermittent bear cycles. Just look at the Dow Jones since its inception. However, even assuming crypto's continued and fruitful existence, a HODLer is still missing the ability to capitalize on the bearish downturns and swings, many lasting months or even years, resulting in catastrophic losses. A HODLer who is also a proficient trader has the ability to maximize profit during all market conditions, enhancing short-term and long-term capital gains along the way.

Crypto goes through viscous market cycles where all too often new market participants enter the game at the wrong time. Newcomers routinely join during the peak of a bull run when excitement is euphoric, the headlines are hyperbolic, and the charts are ripe for profit taking to those who got in early. The implosions, however, can be long-lasting. Undeniably, if you bought the 2017-2018 crypto top, with many altcoins down 90-98%, you would still be HODLing at a massive loss today. To put a 98% loss into perspective, a decline in asset value from $1 to $.02 per coin would take 4,900% to regain the all-time high. Notably, 2017 was not the first occurrence of such a steep or enduring crypto collapse. Even buying midway through a bearish cycle can be excruciatingly painful because, as you will learn later, even the smallest common chart patterns like pennants and flags tend to drop an asset's value by 30-40% in a matter of days.

Thus, learning to trade is all about timing and patience. Crypto has very profitable periods and very painful periods, and the goal here is to weather both and come out with heavy pockets. Not only can a trader capitalize on the downturns and swings, but a trader who understands market behavior and technical analysis can also time their entries, seeking only to enter markets in areas of maximum financial opportunity. This takes patience because the best time to enter a market is often when nobody else wants to. But this doesn't mean every time the market goes down, it's a good entry!

If you HODL, do it wisely! Don't simply accept every punishment the crypto markets deal. **Learn to trade, capitalize on different market conditions, take profit, and protect yourself from market annihilation.** I am not anti-HODL, merely "anti-HODL at all costs and to my own unnecessary financial detriment." I consider HODLing a long-term (multi-year) investment portfolio of very reasonable size, given the high risk and in light of your individual financial situation, to be an acceptable part of a long-term trade strategy.

Still, most of my profit remains in dollars with the goal of accumulating more dollars. As of yet, fiat currencies are still what pays the bills. If you are a HODLer looking to trade or are new to crypto and decide to take the road of both a trader and HODLer, I suggest you pay particular attention to Chapter 12 near the end of the handbook on Fundamental Analysis, Averaging Down, and Hedging. For everyone else, the techniques taught in this handbook cater toward swing and position traders who hold positions open over the course of days, weeks, or months. Don't worry, I define the different types of traders in detail in subsequent sections.

CHAPTER 2:
USING EXCHANGES AND WALLETS

Tokens vs. Coins

Technically, not all cryptos are considered coins. Rather, they are either tokens or coins. A coin is a crypto with its own native blockchain and may be actively mined or pre-mined at launch. A token is issued on a blockchain but is not the native coin of that blockchain. For example, the Ethereum blockchain hosts hundreds of "ERC-20" tokens issued for ICOs and other purposes, but Ethereum is the native coin. Bitcoin is of course a coin. The easy way to remember the difference is each blockchain issuing a crypto only has one coin and may have many tokens.

Exchanges

An exchange is a trading platform where market participants can buy, sell, or otherwise speculate on a crypto. Similar to a stockbroker, the often-centralized platform offers a medium of exchange where buyers can post their "bids" and sellers can list their "offers." Exchanges vary widely depending on target audience, but for the purpose of trading, I will focus only on exchanges that cater toward technical traders rather than "buy and hold" retail investors. Traders will likely need to use more than one exchange if they want to enjoy the full diversity of assets traded across the space. Moreover, different exchanges offer different methods of trading. To utilize the full spectrum of speculative tools, a trader may also need to use various exchanges. Thus, in this handbook, I mention numerous exchanges and equip a new trader with the skills necessary to trade seamlessly between them.

Exchanges should be both liquid (supported by substantial buyers, sellers, and market makers to ensure market stability and the ability to exchange large sums of a crypto) and ideally have a reputation for safety and care for user funds. Each trader must decide for themselves what exchange to use and what is an acceptable risk. I implore each trader to research exchanges heavily before using them as no exchange in crypto is completely fail safe. Below, I highlight a few exchanges based on different use cases.

Binance.com is the largest exchange in the world. Binance offers hundreds of trading pairs, margin (leverage) trading, and high liquidity. Binance also has a notable reputation for user care since it was hacked for $40,000,000 and ensured no users suffered a loss.[i] The wide variety of markets and speculative tools make Binance a one-stop shop for many traders.

Traders interested in small-cap cryptos that aren't utter garbage may want to consider Kucoin.com. Kucoin is the only low-cap exchange I support because they do their homework on vetting projects and offer a multi-step security process, which makes the exchange feel "safer." However, I am not a security expert. Notably, liquidity for some market pairs on Kucoin will be low because many of the coins have tiny market capitalizations and are equivalent to penny stocks. Only use this exchange if you intend to trade its unique array of quality low caps as its liquidity for large-caps is pretty low. If you are interested in trading small-cap coins, make sure to read the sections on altcoin trading and low-cap trading carefully in Part III of this handbook.

Lastly, I will mention Bitmex.com here, with a caveat, because it offers the easiest and one of the most liquid margin trading platforms in the world. A user can easily sign-up with just an email address, deposit Bitcoin, and begin trading with leverage in minutes. Traders are warned Bitmex has a mixed reputation and suffers frequently from issues like slippage, which I define and go into in detail in subsequent sections. Still, Bitmex is a margin trader favorite. I caution it should be used with care and only by experienced traders or only on testnet by inexperienced traders. By far, it has the most casino-like feel and is designed to make you feel pressure to keep trading. So, be warned, it's not a good place to learn to trade responsibly. If you decide to use Bitmex, never make trades based on opinions in the troll box!

Legal Compliance on Exchanges: KYC and AML

You will notice on many exchanges new accounts are limited in what they can trade if they have not gone through legal compliance steps like Know Your Customer (KYC) and Anti-Money Laundering (AML) registration. This requires the user to submit identification like a passport or national ID, current billing receipt confirming residence, and a current photo of the registrant. However, if a user does not wish to submit such information, they may still be allowed to trade but will be subject to a daily withdrawal limit. For example, on Binance or Kucoin, an unregistered account is limited to withdrawing two bitcoins' worth of value in a twenty-four-hour period. Many traders find it acceptable to trade without registration and do not have a problem with only being able to move ~$20,000 or so each day.

Depending on various geographic jurisdictions, customers may also be barred from participating on an exchange. For example, citizens of the United States are not allowed to trade on major exchanges like Binance (with the exception of Binance.us) or Bitmex as this goes against the Terms and Policies of these exchanges. Whether this is widely respected is another question and is not a subject of this handbook. But users should familiarize themselves with the Terms and Policies of the exchanges they choose to use. If a user violates such policies, they may risk their accounts being frozen, funds being lost, or other consequences.

Two-Factor Authentication

Critical to traders, is the use of two-factor authentication (2FA). For those unfamiliar, 2FA provides an additional step of security by requiring, in addition to a login password, a string of numbers provided concurrently either through email, text, or applications like Google Authenticator. Different users may prefer different methods; however, I prefer not to use any email address as a form of 2FA when given the option of text or Google Authenticator. You can activate 2FA on many exchanges by going into the account settings or security settings sections.

Wallets and Transactions

Like a bank account, each crypto trader needs a digital wallet to store their asset(s). Each blockchain requires its own unique wallet. Wallets are easily generated and come with both a public and private key required to receive and send transactions. Similar to a bank routing and account number, an "address," derived from the public key, is comprised of numbers and letters, which users can share with each other to receive funds. The private key is the permission key used to send crypto from that address and should never be shared. Transactions occur when one user sends another user, on the same blockchain, a crypto from wallet one to wallet two. Traders must familiarize themselves with sending and receiving transactions, which I discuss in the next few sections.

Exchange Wallets

As briefly introduced, owning a cryptocurrency requires each user to possess a wallet in which to store it. Exchanges offer all users unique wallets to store each individual crypto sold on that exchange. This creates a frictionless system where traders can deposit, withdraw, buy, and sell hundreds of different cryptos without worrying about how or where to store them. However, as detailed below, a general practice in the space is to keep positions or holdings not anticipated to be sold anytime soon off of the exchanges so as to mitigate risk.

Paramount to the ethos of many cryptocurrency market participants is the idea that each person is their own banking entity in control of their own funds. The community has a saying, "not your keys, not your Bitcoin" (or crypto). This means that if you are not in possession of your own private keys issued to each unique wallet, then you do not actually possess your crypto. Thus, if you hold your cryptocurrency in the wallet of an exchange, they are in control of the wallet's keys, and, consequently, your funds. Accordingly, you subject your assets to the risks associated with that exchange, so you must choose your exchanges carefully.

Exchanges have a long history of hacks and thefts resulting in significant losses to users who trusted them. The most famous hack was Mt. Gox in 2013, where 740,000 bitcoins (current value more than $6 billion) were stolen.[ii] To this day, litigation is ongoing to get user funds back. Since Mt. Gox, dozens of exchanges have suffered hacks. In 2019 alone, some of crypto's most popular and largest exchanges like Binance, Bithumb, and Cryptopia were hacked for tens of millions of dollars.[iii] Cryptopia went bankrupt as a result.[iv]

Unfortunately, as traders we must subject ourselves to the risk of using exchanges. Thus, it's vital to pick them carefully. For the purpose of trading, exchange wallets will suffice because a trader needs to be able to sell a position quickly if it sours. However, whenever possible a trader should consider keeping all unnecessary funds off exchanges.

Decentralized Exchanges

Decentralized exchanges (DEXs) exist where users are supposed to be able to trade without trusting and risking their assets on a centralized exchange, for example, the ability to trade directly from a personal wallet or cold storage device. To date, of the numerous platforms claiming to be decentralized, none in my opinion are ready for serious technical trading. They either lack trading pairs, lack sufficient liquidity to trade effectively, or lack the tools necessary to trade technically, and several have centralized components. One day, however, when truly ready to compete with centralized exchanges, a DEX would be an ideal solution for risk management and technical trading.

Cold Storage Devices

In layman's terms, a cold storage device is a hardware chip similar to a USB, but designed for security, that holds crypto wallets and their keys off-line for users. One device can host numerous unique wallets for dozens of different cryptos and is backed up by a single seed phrase generated when the user activates the device. This seed phrase must be guarded in paper form and should never be shared, photographed, emailed, or otherwise uploaded to a computer or you risk having it discovered and your funds lost. Anyone who has this seed will be able to access your funds.

To access the cold storage wallets, a user merely plugs in the device like a USB chip and follows the instructions provided by the manufacturer. For example, a Trezor device requests the user's numeric pin number, and, when signing into the device, the user must enter their pin using a rotating number pad. Devices generally have their own software with a wallet interface accessible on the manufacturing company's website. Still, wallets may also be linked to third-party services like Myetherwallet.com, which is commonly used to access Ethereum-based wallets from various cold storage devices. Keep in mind, an Ethereum-based wallet can hold any ERC token and thus one wallet can store hundreds of different tokens. One device can also hold many different Ethereum addresses.

Numerous cold storage devices exist, but I only use those from the most reputable manufacturers. For example, a Ledger, Trezor, or KeepKey device. Never buy a device secondhand and always buy it directly from the manufacturer. Each device has a tamperproof seal showing it has not been used. If you buy a used or fake device or get tricked into using fake software, you risk losing your funds to a compromised device. Lastly, before purchasing, users should research what cryptos are supported by each device as some devices provide more options than others.

All serious crypto traders should own a cold storage device to store holdings they are not actively trading. The process of moving funds to cold storage takes mere minutes by making a simple withdrawal from any exchange, which I cover in the next section. Your device can receive funds regardless of whether it's plugged in, but, to move funds out, it must be connected and the security procedures of that device to make a withdrawal must be followed.

Funding an Account, Deposits, and Withdrawals

Before you can trade, you must familiarize yourself with the process of moving money and assets between exchanges and your wallets. When introducing new users to the world of crypto, this area tends to highlight a significant flaw in user experience. It's challenging and not always intuitive for new users. Not all exchanges allow users to deposit directly from their bank account, so this process is often two steps: 1) deposit money from a bank account to a retail-focused "buy and hold" exchange like Coinbase, Gemini, or another widely trusted exchange in your country; and 2) purchase a major crypto like Bitcoin, Ethereum, or a stable coin from that exchange and move it over to a technical trading exchange like Binance, Kucoin, Kraken, or Bittrex. Some exchanges allow for you to "buy" crypto using a credit card, but this may have strong limitations, fees, or otherwise not be possible for many traders.

To make a deposit or withdrawal of a crypto, look for the "Wallet," "Deposit," or "Withdrawal" tabs, which are frequently located on the top navigation bar of the exchange website. Then select the crypto you would like to send and input the address and amount. When you are making a deposit or withdrawal, treat it with the same care as you would if you were making a bank deposit or withdrawal. When sending or receiving, it's critical a user copies the address of the correct cryptocurrency. For example, if you are depositing Bitcoin, you MUST be depositing to a Bitcoin address. If you make a mistake, you will lose your money. I do not suggest sending Bitcoin ever if you can avoid it because Bitcoin is slow and can take hours to arrive. Many stable coins (USDT, PAX, USDC) or altcoins like Ethereum, Litecoin, and XRP may be sent quickly between all major exchanges. Again, always double check and make sure you are sending the right crypto to the right address.

Stable Coins

A stable coin is a crypto token designed to always maintain a stable value based on a government-issued fiat currency (i.e. dollars, euros, yen, yuan, etc.). Stable coins allow fluid trading between cryptos on exchanges without having to constantly shift fiat money back and forth between bank accounts and exchanges. The concept behind a stable coin is each coin stays pegged to the value of one dollar, or other fiat currency, and each coin is fully backed by a real dollar held by the company offering the stable coin. So, traders can easily buy or sell a crypto using a stable coin and not have to convert the proceeds into fiat right away. Notably, while stable coins exist for other fiat currencies like euros or yuan, the most common ones are dollar backed.

Moreover, traders can seamlessly send stable coins to other exchanges because they are tokens issued on various blockchains. For example, Tether (USDT) offers tokens on the Ethereum, Omni, and Tron blockchains, whereas Paxos (PAX) is an Ethereum ERC-20 token. A trader can even send these stable coins to their own cold storage device and truly act as their own bank. This is a key strategy for traders who don't plan on using the funds soon and want to ensure funds are autonomous and safe from exchange hacks or other flaws.

Some stable coins have a long history of suspicion. Famously, the largest stable coin, Tether, has been accused of market manipulation and of not harboring sufficient assets to back the USDT tokens, claims they vehemently deny. Ongoing litigation is currently fighting such accusations in court.[v] Importantly, I suggest traders research every stable coin very carefully and decide what the best choice is for themselves. Several including Paxos (PAX) and USDC have registered with regulators to try to demonstrate their trustworthiness.[vi] I prefer to only use stable coins that make an effort to work with regulators or current regulations.

One of the shortcomings of stable coin choices is the lack of cryptocurrencies paired with the less popular ones or the lack of liquidity traded against less popular ones. By far, Tether has the most crypto pairings on major exchanges and its pairs are often the most liquid. In other words, you can buy or sell the most cryptos using Tether and those markets are supported by a thick volume of buyers and sellers compared to some of Tether's smaller competition. However, I prefer not to hold Tether for long periods of time because I am unsure how I feel about their business. So, I generally trade my USDT for PAX or USDC if I don't plan on using it straight away. Generally, you can trade all one-dollar-backed stable coins for each other at a near 1:1 ratio. After all, they should each represent a single dollar backed by a single dollar's worth of assets.

CHAPTER 3:
TRADER TERMINOLOGY AND
TRADE EXECUTION

Circulating Supply, Price, & Market Capitalization

This section is extremely important for new traders. All new traders MUST understand the differences between asset price, circulating supply, and market capitalization! Asset price is the current value of one unit of the asset. For example, one bitcoin may cost $5,000 or one Ethereum $150. Circulating supply is the total number of units of that coin or token available and circulating in the world with the potential to be sold on exchanges. Market capitalization is the total value of all coins or tokens in circulation.

These definitions are extremely important. Not understanding them may confuse a new trader on the value of what they are purchasing. For example, someone may think one Tron is cheap because its price is .01USD and "it could easily go to $1." However, if Tron has 66,000,000,000,000 coins circulating, and its market cap is thus six hundred and sixty million dollars, it may not be so "cheap" and it would take many billions of dollars of new capital inflow to realize a $1 asset value and market capitalization of sixty-six billion dollars. A 100x gain is not unheard of in crypto but it's also not a walk in the park. Thus, asset price should always be viewed relative to its circulating supply and market capitalization.

Moreover, new traders should be wary of the difference between circulating supply and the potential supply. Many cryptos have a smaller circulating supply that may only represent a tiny fraction of the total supply. For instance, in the example above, Tron has roughly ninety-nine billion coins and only sixty-six billion in circulation. This means nearly thirty billion more will still be distributed into the market. Hedera Hashgraph (HBAR) also comes to mind for this example, but literally dozens if not hundreds of coins and tokens share this concern. HBAR has roughly two billion coins in circulation. However, their coin release schedule will increase that number to fifty billion coins over the next fifteen years as HBARs are released to early investors.[vii] This means if you buy HBAR today, 95% of the supply has yet to be flooded onto the market and the increasing supply could greatly affect future value. While this distinction may be more important for buy and hold investors, it's critical for traders to also understand what they are trading. Things like supply increases may substantially impact an open position.

An opposing but relevant example is Bitcoin halving. In May 2020, the block reward for Bitcoin halved resulting in miners receiving only half as many bitcoins as they did previously for solving each block. A trader and investor may be very interested in the implications this has on the market because it reduces the influx of supply on the market and increases cost of production of a single bitcoin.

Finally, traders should be curious about the percentage of an asset held by its founding organizations or companies. Some companies hold a majority of an asset's supply with the ability to swell the floating circulation immensely. For instance, popular company Ripple and its founders started with 100 billion XRP coins and over the years have sold roughly forty billion of them,[viii] creating constant sell pressure on the market. Consider possible implications of founding organization or companies when they decide to unload assets on the open market. I generally do not trade assets where the teams or founding organizations horde or control the supply.

Types of Traders

Traders are often categorized by the time frames in which they trade. The common categories of traders are day traders, scalp traders, swing traders, and position traders. The particular trade strategies I teach generally cater to swing traders or position traders, which entails traders holding a position open for days, weeks, or even many months and trades on patterns and signals that form over a substantial period of time.

Day traders traditionally trade intra-day market movements and close their positions by the end of the day. Hence, the term "day" trading. This is because stock markets have an open and close time, but in the crypto markets we don't have this limitation. Our markets run 24/7, 365 days a year. A day trader looks to make a quick return on price action that occurs over a short period of time and generally they examine price action under short time frames like 15M, 30M, 1H, and 2H, which I go into further detail in Part II on Technical Analysis. Despite not meeting the strict definition of day trader, many crypto traders still consider themselves to be day trading even if that means they are up at 3am to make a trade.

A scalp trader plays on even smaller time frames than a day trader and may play a chart minute-by-minute. They look to make quick plays off of micro movements in a market. A swing trader positions themselves on trades that may last several days or weeks. Finally, a position trader trades with the intent to hold the position open for many weeks, months, or even years – capitalizing on the long-term movements of an asset rather than concerning themselves with the short-term movements.

My trade strategy avoids short time frame trades and bets on longer-term chart development because I notice lesser degrees of accuracy with technical indicators and analysis on lower time frames. Therefore, I do not recommend new traders start by scalp trading or day trading. However, I often follow short time frame setups and practice on them hypothetically as a way to observe price action and watch the elements of technical analysis play out in real time. If you are interested in trading shorter time frames, the technical analysis taught still applies. But you should be prepared for faster market movements and open positions will take a greater degree of caution, care, and monitoring.

If you've ever watched the news, you've probably heard the terms bull and bear markets. Simply stated, a bull market is a market where the buyers are in control and a bear market is a market where the sellers are in control. Generally, bull and bear markets show a sustained trend over months or years. Market participants betting the price of an asset will go up are referred to as the bulls because bulls buck their horns upward in a fight. Market participants betting the price of an asset will go down are called bears because bears paw and claw in a downward motion in a fight. If someone say they are bullish on an asset, they are saying they think its price will rise. If someone says they are bearish, they are saying they think the price will fall.

Importantly, during a bull market, there will be many "dips" and downturns but a key aspect is the general price action continues to make higher high points and lows tend to trend higher. Conversely, in a bear market, there will be spikes and bounces but the general price action continues to make lower high points and lower lows.

A widely accepted definition of when a market switches from one to another, among stock traders, is a gain or loss beyond 20% of market index's recent value. For example, a bull market may emerge when, during a downtrend, a stock market index gains 20% of value since its bottom low, while a bear market may emerge when a stock market index loses more than 20% from its high. This definition, however, is more applicable to stock markets rather than crypto because crypto assets regularly move 20% in a single day. Moreover, even applying this definition in the stock market could be troublesome. Take for example the recent stock plunge due to the coronavirus Stock indexes dropped 30% and then bounced more than 20%. News outlets like the Wall Street Journal applying this classic definition were eager to say stocks were back in a bull market and just a week after declaring a bear market.[ix] Applying this classic definition so rigidly may cause confusion with investors. In the case of the Wall Street Journal, it may even be reckless as they lead their readers into thinking the markets are a safe buy again in bull territory when they may not be. Sometimes you just won't know whether the market has switched from bearish to bullish or bullish to bearish until substantially after the fact. I generally look to the volatility beyond one major move and see whether the trend of lows and highs changes course.

Buying and Selling vs. Longing and Shorting

While many crypto traders use the terms "buying" and "longing" or "shorting" and "selling" interchangeably, it's important to note how these terms can be used differently. To buy a crypto means to actually buy the asset and hold it in a wallet. Similarly, to sell an asset means to rid yourself of the possession of that asset through its sale either for another asset, fiat money, or a stable coin.

Many traders will say they are "long" on an asset when they buy it, which generally is accepted. But, one can go long on Bitcoin or other cryptos without purchasing the underlying asset through derivatives like options (right-to-buy-later), swaps (agreement to exchange instruments), or futures (obligation-to-buy-later). To go long on a crypto generally means you are betting that a crypto will increase in price and you have an expectation of profit by selling your position on that asset at a later time. This could be achieved by either selling the actual asset for a profit (if you purchased the asset itself) or by closing a position that bet on the asset's rise when the price increases. For example, if you bet on Bitcoin going up through a futures contract and you sell your position before the expiry date.

However, the same interchangeability is not as commonly said for the terms "short" and "selling." Selling requires a trader own the asset and dispose of it whereas a short means a trader makes a bet, generally on loan,[1] that an asset will go down. When someone says they are "short" on a crypto this means they are literally betting against the price rise of the crypto; they are betting the price of that crypto will go down. Whereas

---

[1] **Note:** A short often works by a trader borrowing or buying an asset on loan, selling it, then rebuying it lower, returning the loaned asset or funds, and profiting from the difference. However, this process is often streamlined/automated and the short position is often displayed in a position that reflects the profits from this series of actions. I.e. asset price goes down, short trade value goes up; or asset price goes up, short trade value goes down.

if someone "sells" their crypto, they lock in a capital gain or loss but, unlike a short, they have no expectation of profiting further if the crypto they sold goes down. A seller may be waiting to rebuy lower or may later decide to do so, which may act effectively similar to a short. However, unlike a short, selling a crypto does not compel a loss or potential liquidation if an asset rises against the position.

To put this into context, an easy example is the Bitmex perpetual Bitcoin swap. Traders use Bitcoin to bet in favor of (long) or against (short) the future value of Bitcoin. Traders buy and sell swap contracts (valued in USD) against each other asserting either the price will go up or the price will go down. If the price goes up, the shorts pay the longs. If the price goes down, the longs pay the shorts. It's sort of like an endless Conga Line Dance where participants hop on and off and have to settle their wins or losses as they leave the dance.

What's a Squeeze?

You have probably heard someone on television, a podcast, or the radio talk about a squeeze when referring to stocks on the evening news. A squeeze occurs when a market moves in the opposite direction of a market participant such that the market participant is forced to close their position and buy or sell. In a short squeeze, short sellers are compelled to close their positions and purchase an asset because the market is rising against their position squeezing them out of it. This further drives the price of an asset up. In a long squeeze, the contrary is true, and buyers are compelled to sell their positions because the market is going down – squeezing them out of it. This further drives the value of the asset down.

Margin (Leverage) vs. Spot Trading

You will hear traders frequently use the terms "margin" and "spot" trading. For instance, a trader may say they are "spot-long" or "margin-long." The difference is simple: a spot order is one where the trader buys the asset from their own funds, while a margin order is where the asset is speculated on through a loan. With margin, a trader can long or short more of an asset than they could normally afford by leveraging the funds they have as collateral for a larger trade. In other words, margin is the amount of fiat money or an asset (i.e. Bitcoin) required to open or keep open a leveraged trade. Say I have a $1,000 balance, but I want to bet $10,000 on Bitcoin going up. I can do this by making a borrowed order (on margin) using 10x leverage. The lender (often the exchange), will put out the additional $9,000 I need to make the trade. This means, however, that my balance will lose value at ten times the rate it normally would if I did not leverage the trade. So, a 10% decline in Bitcoin's value would wipe me out. Often, on margin, when you lose the value of your balance (including any fees/interest paid), in this case $1,000, the trade gets liquidated, the lender is repaid, and all funds are lost. It's important to read and understand the differing rules and debt obligations for each exchange before margin trading.

Some exchanges that offer margin trading will only allow 5x leverage, while others like Bitmex offer 100x leverage or even 125x leverage at Binance. Importantly, NO TRADER new or experienced, should ever use anything close to 50x, 100x, or 125x leverage. You will get liquidated with the smallest market move, and the probability of timing a trade with such precision is so low it reduces the "trade" to mere gambling, and very poorly favored gambling at that. Many experienced traders when trading on margin use only 2-5x leverage.

How to Execute a Buy and Sell Order

When you are ready to make your first trade, how do you execute it? On exchanges designed for a basic buy and hold investors, there is likely just a simple "Buy" or "Sell" button. However, as a technical trader you must be familiar with several types of orders and how to execute them. A trader must know how and when to use limit orders, stop-limit orders, market orders, and stop-market orders. To execute a trade, head over to a "Markets" section of an exchange and select a crypto you would like to trade. All exchanges display some variation of a chart; an order book with unfilled bids and offers; and a section to select, input, and execute a trade.

Limit Orders

The limit order is your standard buy and sell order where you set the bid or offer price. If the bid price is below the current price of the asset, then it will add your order to the existing order book. Similarly, if your sell offer is above the current trading price, then it will add your offer to the sell side of the order book. Your limit order will execute when the price reaches that point and when sellers sell into your bid or buyers buy into your offer. Keep in mind, other traders will have offers or bids at the same price that need to be filled too.

For example, if Bitcoin is trading at $5,000 but you think it will go down and you want to buy at $4,500, you can place your limit order bid for $4,500. Or, if Bitcoin is trading at $5,000 and you are looking to sell but you think it will go up to $5,500 first, you can place a limit sell order for $5,500.

A limit order will execute immediately if you place a bid above the current trading price or sell offer below the current trading price. For example, if Bitcoin is trading at $5,000 and you place a limit order bid at $5,001, your order will execute and fill to the extent there are sellers with offers at $5,001. Conversely, if Bitcoin is trading at $5,000 and you place a limit order sell at $4,999 your sell order will execute to the extent there are buyers with bids at $4,999. You may wish to place a limit order some value farther above or below the current trading price to ensure it fills (i.e. $5,050 or $4,950). Your limit order will fill at the earliest price where there is liquidity.

Stop-Limit Orders

The stop-limit order is a conditional order that allows to you to set a limit order upon an asset reaching a future price. For your limit order to be placed, the stop price must be hit. You add an extra condition ("stop") to the equation telling the exchange when you want it to place your order. To make this order you give the exchange two inputs: 1) the stop price to trigger the order, and 2) the limit price (bid or offer) where you want to buy or sell. The limit price should never be greater than your bottom line for where you want to buy or sell an asset. Still, you want to place your limit order such that it has a high chance of execution. The stop-limit order gives a trader the greatest control over a trade that cannot simply be input as a simple bid or offer (limit).

For example, if Bitcoin is at $5,000 and I expect the price to breakout and accelerate if it breaches $5,100, then I can place a stop-limit order at $5,101, telling the exchange to set a limit buy at $5,125. Upon $5,101 being hit my order will be placed and will execute and fill so long as sellers have offers at $5,125 or below. The reason why I would not just put a stop-limit order at $5,102 is because if the price accelerates too quickly my order may be skipped if there are insufficient offers for me to buy at $5,102. My order may very well fill at $5,102 or at the lowest price where my bid can be filled, but I'm giving the exchange some latitude to ensure it fills. A simple way of thinking about this is setting your limit input for the maximum price you are willing to purchase an asset at.

As another example, if Bitcoin is $5,000 but I expect the price to fall sharply if it breaks down below $4,950, I can set a stop-limit order telling the exchange to place a sell order upon hitting $4,949. My stop price would be $4,949 and I could set my limit price at $4,925. Thus, I would be willing to sell my bitcoin to anyone bidding as low as $4,925 upon the break of $4,949. Ideally, I would hope my sells get filled higher, at $4,949, but this allows some wiggle room.

Market Orders

A market order is an order that executes a buy or sell at the earliest market price. It will match your bid or sell offer to the closest opposing bid or offer without restriction. This order sacrifices specificity and caution for ease of use. While this is the easiest order to use, I think traders should rarely, if ever, use a market order. Market orders can easily cause you to enter an immediate losing position if the market is moving quickly.

Stop-Market Orders

Finally, the stop-market order is the conditional version of the market order. Similar to a stop-limit order you input a stop price for your market order to trigger. However, rather than placing a limit on the price you are willing to buy or sell at, the order executes against the earliest opposing bids and offers without restriction.

For example, if Bitcoin is trading at $5,000 and I think it will have an explosive move upward if it breaks above $5,100, then I could put a stop-market buy order for $5,101. However, this could be an extremely risky move. If I am so convinced the price of Bitcoin will explode above $5,100, then I should be cautious about where my market order will execute. Often times, upon a big breakout, the price of Bitcoin can rise sharply and I may get an order filled substantially higher than what I was expecting. This is what we call slippage, which I go into more detail on in the sections below.

To be frank, with few exceptions, stop-market orders are used by amateurs who don't know the smarter way to trade. You can fulfill the same purpose but with far less risk using the stop-limit order. The stop-limit order lets you decide for yourself what an acceptable amount of slippage is and will not execute an order that will harm you beyond the conditions you have pre-determined.

Stop-Loss

A stop-loss is an order set by a trader to close a position when their trade goes south. A stop-loss can be a stop-market order or a stop-limit order, which closes at a future price to mitigate losses or secure gains. For example, if I buy a bitcoin for $5,000 but I think that if it goes below $4,900 it will crash. I will set stop-loss order for below $4,899 to sell my bitcoin and exit my position. If I were short, I would set a stop-loss at an acceptable point of loss above where I entered. I suggest using a stop-loss for every trade that is not a long-term position trade where you are hoping to capitalize over many weeks or months. Consider the parameters of your stop-loss carefully. If you place a stop-loss too low, it may cause an unacceptable loss if triggered. However, a stop-loss too close to an entry may get triggered on a small countermove before an asset continues the way you were thinking.

Slippage

Slippage is a term coined for when a market quickly moves up or down with insufficient liquidity causing traders' positions to be skipped or orders to be executed significantly above or below where a trader anticipates. For example, say Bitcoin is trading at $5,000 and you unwisely place a stop-market short order at or below $4,800 because you think if Bitcoin breaks below that level it will dump. As it turns out, you are right! However, everyone else thinks so too and the market cannot support the amount of selling at that level and quickly drops to $4,650 where your market order finally executes before recovering back to $4,800. You have just been a victim of slippage and your short is already substantially underwater. Unfortunately, slippage is very common on leverage exchanges and should be anticipated frequently.

One way to avoid significant slippage is by using stop-limit orders delineating the maximum range you are willing to enter the trade. Your order may be skipped and not filled if the market slips quickly below your limit range but at least you will not be a victim to a market order executing far below where you anticipated.

Finally, account for slippage when closing a trade as well. For instance, if you have a short in play but the market is rising if you have your stop-loss set as a stop-market order, you risk your short getting closed unacceptably higher than you anticipate. However, if slippage causes your stop-limit stop-loss order to be skipped you may suffer the same outcome or even liquidation. This is why traders need to carefully account for slippage and be careful with high leverage trades. Unfortunately, slippage is an issue that cannot be completely avoided, particularly if you margin trade.

Hidden Orders and Spoofing

Many exchanges allow for hidden orders. A hidden order is an order you will not see on the order book and is intentionally hidden by the buyer or seller. Hidden orders may be used when someone wants to accumulate or discard a lot of a crypto without letting the market know. For instance, if a trader posts a large bid or offer (often called a "buy wall" or "sell wall") it may influence other traders to buy or sell because they see someone is looking to accumulate or unload a large quantity of an asset. This can be counter-productive to the posting trader because it may cause their bid or offer to be out paced by tagalongs. Thus, by hiding the order, a fat pocket trader can accumulate or discard a crypto without influencing the market.

"Spoofing" is a widely illegal market manipulation where a trader intentionally puts up fake buy or sell walls to influence the market. A spoofer will remove the buy or sell wall when traders start to consume it because they do not actually want to take that position. Often the ill-intentioned trader will make orders in the opposite direction of where they want the market to go. For instance, a spoofer may put up big orders on the buy side to create the illusion of strong demand with the hope the price will go up. This may be because the culprit genuinely wants to push the market up or they may have sales offers they want to drive the price into. Similarly, such a trader may put spoof sell orders to drive the price down. This may be done to accumulate and fill bids or simply to manipulate the market lower to power a pre-existing position.

Spoofing is extraordinarily common in crypto. If you are trading on a leverage exchange like Bitmex, it's important not to give much, if any, weight to the order book. You may see millions of contracts "supporting" the price when they will just disappear in a minute or two. Never trade off of existing orders. Consult the chart and apply the techniques of technical analysis. *As a general rule, the order books cannot be trusted and do not accurately and consistently indicate the future movement of the asset.*

Exchange Fees and Tips for Reducing Them

Traders should be mindful of the varying fees at the exchanges they trade. Some exchanges like Coinbase and Gemini for "buy and hold" investors charge insane rates as much as 1-2% per trade. On technical exchanges like Binance, Bitmex, Kucoin, Bittrex or many others the rates will be lower. However, traders are cautioned that different types of orders may trigger different exchange fees. Fortunately, a few easy tips can help you save hard earned money over time.

First, numerous exchanges offer fee discounts if you hold that exchange's native coin or token and the exchange may charge you their coin when you execute a trade. For instance, holding Binance Coin (BNB) on Binance or Kucoin Shares (KCS) on Kucoin. Putting a small amount of money into an exchange coin where you trade frequently can help you save on fees over time.

Second, watch out for fees on leverage exchanges and know how to take advantage of them. For instance, if you trade on Bitmex and decide to market order with leverage you will be charged the % in fees based on the number of contracts you order irrespective of what it cost you on margin. In other words, if you leverage $1,000 worth of Bitcoin at 10x to buy $10,000 contracts, you will be charged the exchange fee ($10,000 x .075% = $7.50). To avoid this, rather than market ordering you can set a limit order (not one that will execute immediately but one that adds to the order book) and check the "Post-Only" box, which allows you to receive the market maker rebate. Users applying the rebate receive a .025% rebate (.025% x 10,000 = +$2.5) as a reward for marking making rather than paying the normal .075% fee for market orders.[x] The idea is market makers, not takers, get incentivized for adding to the order books. However, traders on Bitmex should be mindful of its "funding" feature where active positions on the perpetual market pay each other every eight hours depending on Bitmex's two-component calculation (weighing the interest rate and the premium/discount).[xi]

Third, take advantage of promotions for new traders. Many exchanges offer fee discounts and incentives when you sign up for a new account. It's worth scouring the exchanges for promotions before opening an account to see whether you are eligible for one. Also, if you have friends who already trade, perhaps using one of their referral codes would be mutually beneficial.

Trade Execution Takeaways:

1. Trading on "margin" means trading using borrowed funds, while "spot" means using only your own funds. New traders are strongly encouraged to trade spot or, if trading on margin, to use very low leverage.

2. Limit orders should almost always be used over market orders.

3. Traders should watch out for slippage.

4. Traders should ignore the order books because of the risk of spoofing. Consult the charts!

5. Traders should be mindful of exchange fees and know the tools to help mitigate them.

II. TECHNICAL ANALYSIS

The second portion of this handbook is dedicated to learning technical analysis, which is the practice of studying and predicting price action and comprises the skills necessary to be a trader. This particular trading strategy requires combining several methods and techniques of technical analysis. Traders must learn how to read a chart, understand its various moving components, and observe price behavior using several indicators. This includes fluency and mastery of Japanese candlesticks, volume, time frames, trend lines and channels, continuation and reversal chart patterns, the relative strength index (RSI), and divergences. This strategy assesses each chart under the totality of the circumstances. Meaning, different weight might be given to different indications depending on how the chart presents as a whole.

When applying technical analysis, a trader's primary goal should be to *act on a strong inclination that the market will behave a certain way imminently*. Importantly, technical analysis does not guarantee an outcome. Rather, it seeks to find and utilize identifiable and repeating patterns occurring in market price action. In other words, technical analysis merely suggests possibilities to a trader from which they can draw a theory. While no technical indicator is certain, undeniably, in many instances, market behavior repeats itself similarly. These repeating behaviors form the foundation of technical analysis. So, studying previous market behaviors offers insights into common occurrences and potential future market behaviors. Through technical analysis, traders are able to position themselves with a greater understanding of how price action works and how the markets flow. Finally, technical analysis should be construed in light of all other factors, including fundamental analysis, which seeks to find the intrinsic or "fundamental" value of an asset by evaluating the driving forces behind the asset outside of the marketplace. Fundamental analysis is detailed further in Chapter 12 of Part III.

CHAPTER 4:
READING A CHART

Chart Anatomy

Chart reading is a beautiful thing. I'm not kidding. Not only will charting help you understand any global market when you see the swings and dips on the news, but it's also a direct insight into human emotion and the real-time exchange of capital between market participants. A chart is a historical record of capital flow and group psychology, and, in each chart, you can see market moves that made or broke lives. Charts show collective moments of extreme greed, or fear, and offer a means of predicting future movements of price action. Charts are a valuable tool, and becoming a chartist is a skill that often becomes a passion.

What we are looking at when viewing a chart is the value of an asset over time. A technical chart, regardless of whether it's for a crypto, stock, commodity, or any other asset, is defined by its X and Y axes. Always on the X axis is a measurement of time, while on the Y axis is a measurement of value or price. Thus, we are examining value changing over time.

Importantly, a chart is dynamic and must be read as it evolves. A particular disposition of a chart may change as time goes on. Traders should be willing to abandon dispositions if the price action changes course. Charting isn't about proving a pre-existing theory or disposition (although certainly many investors love to charge their bias on an asset using charts). Rather, it's about reading into suggestions on what might come next from a neutral, objective standpoint. You may have a bias and that's okay as a human being, but, as a trader, bias and subjectivity are a danger that can directly interfere with judgment and a successful trade strategy.

When choosing a chart for a particular asset, I always pick one representing data from a major exchange, which preferably has years of chart history for an asset. For example, if looking at Bitcoin I always use the chart from either Coinbase, Bitmex (XBT), or Binance because the price history is substantial, the liquidity of those exchanges is high, and the price action is not as frequently subject to outlier fluctuations that may occur in an illiquid market. Charting becomes very difficult if you have to account for a "flash crash" (a sudden drop or spike in price that's outside the norm of regular price movement). However, Bitmex's XBT still regularly suffers from extreme slippage and should be treated with caution.

The anatomy of a chart consists of numerous variables. Figure 4.1 below will familiarize you with the basic structure of a technical chart on Tradingview, which is the industry standard for technical charting. To access a technical chart, log onto Tradingview.com and search for Bitcoin or another crypto on any major exchange using the search bar. Upon making your selection, you will see a non-technical blue line chart and on the bottom left is a button saying, "Technical Chart." Select that button to access the technical chart and tools necessary to trade.

Please note the attribution below all chart-based images in this handbook stating "(tradingview chart)." This means the charts were created using Tradingview.com. However, the analysis and content modifications are my own, which were created using Tradingview's tools.

Figure 4.1 The anatomy of a chart. (tradingview chart)

1) The X axis with time.

2) The Y axis with price.

3) The name of the asset, its pair, and the exchange.

4) The time frame (in this case 1D), to the left of the time frame is the ticker symbol (ETHUSD), and, to the right, the "f" symbol is the indicators and strategies tool.

5) The trade volume consisting of green and red bars.

6) The location of additional tools/indicators below the primary chart. The RSI is highlighted here.

7) The location for noting indicators at play on the primary chart display such as volume or moving averages.

Logarithmic vs. Linear

When examining a chart, a trader can choose between a logarithmic or linear scale. Because of the extreme volatility of cryptocurrencies, many, if not most traders, prefer to use the log scale. Simply put, the log scale best balances extreme price action relative to the entire historical record and is particularly useful when measuring large or exponential growth. In crypto, with many assets appreciating 1,000-20,000%, sometimes thousands of percentage points in mere days, using the log scale helps balance and fit the extreme volatility. Log charts scale an axis based on a base number rising by powers (logarithms), while the linear scale always gives equal weight to units on an axis and can over emphasize or awkwardly scale recent market moves. To make sure your chart is on the log scale check the bottom right corner of the chart and select log (see Figure 4.2 below).

Figure 4.2 (tradingview excerpt)

Volume

Figure 4.3 An image of trade volume bars cut from a chart. (tradingview excerpt)

When a trader says the word "volume" what they are talking about is the aggregate number of asset units exchanged between buyers and sellers over a period of time. For example, the amount of Bitcoin bought and sold. In crypto, traders frequently speak of volume in terms of dollars. When someone says, "Bitcoin had a forty-billion-dollar volume today" that means forty billion dollars' worth of Bitcoin was bought and sold that day.[2] On a chart, volume is represented over time in red or green bars. If a bar is green, it means that buyers dominated the exchange of the asset during that period. Meaning, more buyers were purchasing from sellers' offers than sellers were selling into buyers' bids. Conversely, if the bar is red, it means sellers dominated the exchange during that period by

---

[2] Whether volume in the crypto markets is accurate is up for debate. "Wash trading" (fake buys and sells executed by the same entity) is suspected of inflating trade volumes on some bad actor exchanges as much as 90%. However, this is improving according to a 2019 Blockchain Transparency Institute Report available at Bti.live.

selling into buyers' bids more than buyers were purchasing their offers. When buyers are in control, the price rises. When sellers are in control, the price falls.

"Low volume" means not a lot of the asset was exchanged at that price range, and the amount of selling or buying it takes to eat through offers or sink bids is small. "High volume" means a lot of an asset was exchanged at that price. A trader may say something like "that was a low volume dump," which means the sellers had control and dropped ("dumped") the price but it wasn't supported by a large exchange of crypto.

Traders often examine volume when determining the strength of a move. Generally, if a significant move up or down comes with high volume, it suggests more power behind the move and vice versa. For instance, a low volume breakout might be viewed skeptically by traders because they may think it's unsustainable and insufficiently supported by buyers.

Volume is also a helpful indicator when looking for tops or bottoms of trends. Often, a top or bottom is accompanied by a large amount of volume exchanged. So, when a trader is trying to determine whether a trend is about to reverse, volume can certainly be a helpful indication. As shown in Figure 4.4 below, large volume sticks repeatedly accompany a major shift in trend.

Moreover, declining volume can indicate that a move (up or down) may be weakening and will not continue. For instance, if sellers dump to a new low and buyers recover the price a bit, but the buy volume is trending down. This may indicate diminishing interest from buyers and their continued ability to push the price further.

Figure 4.4 BTC/USD, 1D, Coinbase (tradingview chart)
Notice how each major high and low point from 2018 into 2020 was accompanied by significant volume.

Time Frames

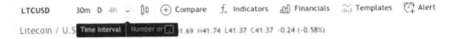

Figure 4.5 An example of time interval selection. (tradingview excerpt)

When examining a chart, a trader must input the time frame (interval) they wish to see the price portrayed. Technical traders frequently use candlestick charts where price action is shown in a string of red and green candles over a period of time. With each candle representing one unit of the selected time frame. The next section below goes over candlesticks in detail. For the purpose of this section, a trader merely needs to understand that when viewing a chart, you are always going to be examining price under a specific time frame.

Some traders only trade higher frame charts represented by four-hour (4H), one-day (1D), or even one-week (1W) candles. Under those settings, price action is delineated in candles that each represent four hours, one day, or one week of trading, respectively. Other traders may look at low time frame candles. For example, a day trader may look at two-hour (2H) one-hour (1H), or 30-minute (30M) candles. A really low time frame scalper may look at a chart minute by minute with 1-minute (1M), 5-minute (5M), 15-minute (15M), and 30-minute (30M) candles. Most importantly, when a trader says they are observing the "daily chart" or "four-hour chart," what they are really saying is they are observing price action with candles delineated in these increments.

What time frame is best depends on what type of trader you are. For my trading strategy, I focus generally on higher frames like 4H and 1D. However, I like to break things into smaller or larger frames for different purposes. As a new trader, I suggest only working trade setups on the 4H and 1D time frames because, as I think you will see, the clearest and most reliable trade signals appear on these larger frames. If you trade on smaller time frames, the signals can become invalided easily and the chart disposition changes more frequently. However, no harm will come from messing with all the different time frames and becoming fluent in all of them. If you apply my performance analysis of chart patterns described later on, you should only apply it to patterns measured on the 1D chart.

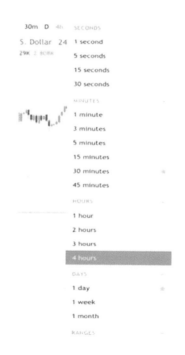

Figure 4.6
(tradingview excerpt)

To select your time frame, hover the mouse over the Time Interval drop down on the top right side of the Tradingview chart.

Tradingview users working with the free content are able to use all frames except the second-by-second frames, which is beyond sufficient to trade this strategy.

Importantly, the crypto markets are 24/7 and unless you are trading futures or on a minority exchange that has time gaps, the chart behavior and candlestick analysis defined in the following sections below may vary from traditional methods and readings on trading stocks or other assets. Figure 4.7 below shows a chart with gaps versus a chart without gaps. For the purpose of this handbook, we will stick to the perpetual markets without gaps because most exchanges/cryptos are displayed this way.

PERPETUAL MARKET (CONTINUOUS WITHOUT GAPS)

FUTURES MARKET (GAPS)

Figure 4.7 (tradingview charts)
An example of a perpetual market chart without gaps next to a futures
market chart with gaps.

CHAPTER 5:
JAPANESE CANDLESTICKS (CRYPTO-
FRIENDLY INTERPRETATION)

Figure 5.1 Candlesticks (tradingview excerpt)

Japanese candlestick trading originated in Japan during the 18th century with commodity traders speculating on the price of rice. The technique's popularity materialized in the West in 1991 when Steve Nison published his book *Japanese Candlestick Charting Techniques.*[xii] Candlestick analysis is a predictive tool used to determine price trends and shifts in trends. Candlesticks show price action during a set period of time and are comprised of "bodies" and "wicks." In this section, you will learn the basics of reading and understanding candlestick chart analysis. *Understand, the candlestick analysis defined below may vary from traditional securities or other teachings because of the perpetual nature of most crypto markets. The formations and patterns are defined from my crypto-centric trader's interpretation. This may offend some purists!*

When reading candlesticks, it's vital to understand how price action forms them. Each candle is a blank canvas that shows the change in value over the time frame examined. For instance, a one-hour (1H) candle shows the price action over one hour. The candle is completely formed at the end of the hour and a new one begins on the new hour. The beginning of the new candle starts with the first transaction of the new period, and whether the candle is green (buyer controlled) or red (seller controlled) is determined by the price of the asset relative to where it began during that period. For example, if Bitcoin is trading at $10,000 when the candle begins (opens) and rises to $10,050 where it ends (closes), the candle will be colored green. Whereas, if Bitcoin closes below $10,000 in that period, it will be colored red. The "body" is the solid colored part of a candle marking the distance between the open and close of the examined period. The greater the distance between open and close, the larger the body.

If an asset gains value and then loses it during a candle's formation period, it creates what is called a wick. The wick is a thin line representing the high or low where the price went before it changed course. Thus, what you are actually observing when a candle forms a wick is a change in who is controlling the price of the asset – either the buyers gained control but later lose control or the sellers gained control but later lose it. Think of trading as a tug of war where buyers and sellers are in constant competition trying to pull the opposition onto their side. Importantly, many traders may use the term "shadow" for wick, and some may only apply the definition of "wick" to the upper part of a candle and use the term "tail" for the bottom. This handbook only uses the term wick and applies it for all purposes mentioned above.

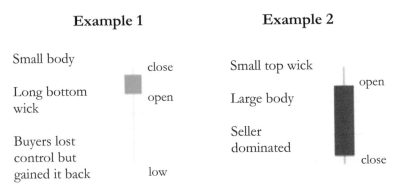

Figure 5.2 (tradingview excerpts)
Examples of two different types of candles: Example 1 with a small body ending with buyers in control and Example 2 with a large body ending with sellers in control.

A trader may examine a chart on multiple time frames to get a better picture of what's going on. For example, a trader might compare the candles on the 1H chart with the 4H chart to examine or break down the price action meticulously. If a 4H chart shows a seller dominated red candle, it may be useful for a trader to see at what point in that four-hour period sellers took control.

Finally, candlestick analysis requires reading strings of candles in conjunction. Understanding what individual candles mean, as well as sets of candles (formations or patterns), can help a trader determine the strength of a trend or when a trend is about to reverse. A nice analogy comes from flowers. An individual flower is identifiable and beautiful in its own way but when grouped together in a cluster or bouquet its beauty and significance are magnified. Flowers can be arranged infinitely together to create different expressions or evoke different emotions – red roses for love, yellow daffodils or sunflowers for happiness, tulips for well-wishes, or a mix of many flowers simply for beauty. Similarly, a candlestick may be appreciated for its suggestion alone, but, when combined with other candlesticks its mere singular suggestion may strengthen in comradery or change completely to evoke a whole new meaning. The following sections identify common candlestick forms and patterns and their potential disposition on the future price movement of an asset.

I caution that candlesticks are a tool that should be read in light of all other aspects of technical analysis. For example, consideration of surrounding candles, trade volume, trend lines, chart patterns, oscillators and momentum gauges like the RSI, or other market signals. Many forms appear during reversals, consolidation periods, and as continuations, so it's vital to understand other aspects of technical analysis. I rarely make a trade based solely on a candlestick formation without some other complementary indicator.

Bullish Candles and Formations

Before looking at particular bullish candles and formations, it's important to note the color of a candle (red or green) does not necessarily implicate whether the candle is bullish or bearish. A bullish candle can indeed be red if it appears at the end of a downtrend. However, in instances where a candle may be bullish regardless of color, some traders may treat green candles with a greater bullish bias because the candle closed above the open. What's most important is understanding how the candle is formed, which can assist you in understanding why it has a bullish or bearish disposition. I note when a candle must be green, for instance, with bullish engulfing candles.

Bullish Spinning Top

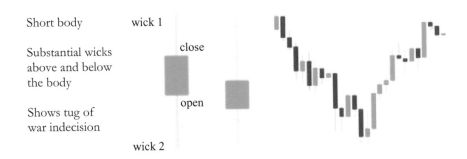

Figure 5.3 (tradingview charts)

The spinning top is a candle with both a substantial upper and lower wick as well as a short body. The body doesn't have to be perfectly centered; however, if it's situated on the top or bottom it may be another candle like a hammer or shooting star. Also, if the body looks more like the cross of a "t," then the candle is likely a doji, which is a relative of the spinning top. Spinning tops appear frequently and show indecision in the market and a period where buyers and sellers each held a dominating position before losing it. Spinning tops appear commonly in times of consolidation, continuation, and reversal. While they are not innately bullish or bearish leaning, a spinning top that occurs after a significant downtrend can mark a shift in the power struggle and indicate a bullish reversal. The color of the candle is determined by who controlled the price action at close of the time period and is not necessarily relevant to determining a bullish disposition. In other words, a red spinning top can be a bullish indicator at the end of a downtrend.

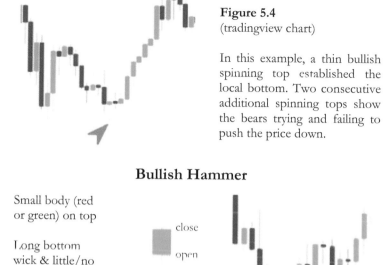

Figure 5.4
(tradingview chart)

In this example, a thin bullish spinning top established the local bottom. Two consecutive additional spinning tops show the bears trying and failing to push the price down.

Bullish Hammer

Small body (red or green) on top

Long bottom wick & little/no wick on top

Buyers lost control but gained it back

close

open

Figure 5.5 (tradingview charts)

The bullish hammer is defined by its long bottom wick and short, wickless or nearly wickless, body at the top, which creates a hammer-like shape. A hammer is formed in a period where sellers take control of an asset dropping its price, but before the defined period of time is over, the buyers take back control and push the price back just above or below the open (creating a green or red candle, respectively). The hammer is a useful tool because it shows the sellers' inability to drive the price of an asset further down and sustain it. A hammer indicates seller exhaustion and commonly signals reversal when it occurs during a downtrend.

Inverted Hammer

Figure 5.6 (tradingview charts)

The inverted hammer is exactly as it sounds – an upside-down hammer. It's defined by its long top wick and lower short body (head), which occurs when the open and close price are very similar but only after the price makes a significant move up before retreating back down near where it started. While this might not sound bullish intuitively because the bears pushed the price down after a rise; the inverted hammer shows the bulls challenging the downtrend and an attempt at reversal. The inverted hammer can be useful as a buy signal and as a signal to the bears hinting they may be losing steam.

Bullish Engulfing Candle

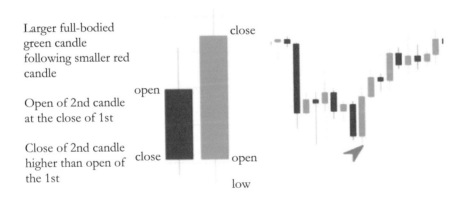

Figure 5.7 (tradingview charts)

A bullish engulfing candle occurs when the body of a larger, buyer dominated, green candle follows a smaller-bodied, seller dominated, red candle. Thus, the body of the green candle completely "engulfs" the preceding red candle without consideration to the wicks. This formation requires the green candle open at the closing price of the red candle and close above the open price of the red candle.

NOTE: Traditionally, a stock trader may say the open of the green candle must be lower than the close of the red candle and gap down; however, as mentioned previously, our markets are 24/7 and do not gap like a stock market does between trading hours. So, look for a candle opening at the same level and engulfing the previous candle.

Bullish Harami

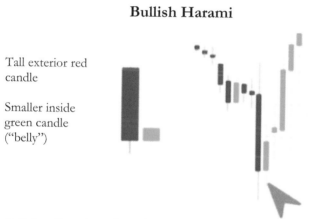

Tall exterior red candle

Smaller inside green candle ("belly")

Figure 5.8 (tradingview charts)

The bullish harami is defined by a larger exterior red candle and a smaller succeeding green candle with its body contained inside the body of the red candle. The word harami comes from a Japanese word for "pregnant," and the candle formation takes its name from the resemblance of the red candle harboring the green candle in its belly. Bullish haramis display a pause in volatility and can indicate that trend reversal is imminent in a downtrend; however, bullish haramis that fail can result in a sharp decline. Thus, many traders wait for confirmation with an additional candle (the three inside up confirmation pattern).

NOTE: Traditionally, traders often require the belly candle of the harami to gap up inside the mother candle's body and some may give more weight to a harami when the belly candle's wicks are completely inside the mother candle's body. However, unless you are trading futures or an exchange that has time frame gaps, as noted in the previous section on time frames, you will not see such a strict definition of a harami in crypto.

Bullish Harami Cross

Large red
outside candle

Inside doji or
thin spinning
top

Figure 5.9 (tradingview charts)

The harami cross is the same thing as a harami except the inside belly candle is either a doji or very thin spinning top, which looks like a cross. Again, since you likely will not be trading gaps in crypto, this example is as close as it gets in a perpetual market. The harami cross signals the same potential bullish reversal. Some traders may give greater weight to a harami cross over a normal harami as a reversal signal.

Three Inside Up (Harami Confirmation)

Figure 5.10 (tradingview charts)

The three inside up pattern is a bullish confirmation pattern following the harami or harami cross. One additional green candle establishes buyer control and confirms the preceding green belly candle. The three inside up is a common entry signal for a trader playing a harami.

Morning Star

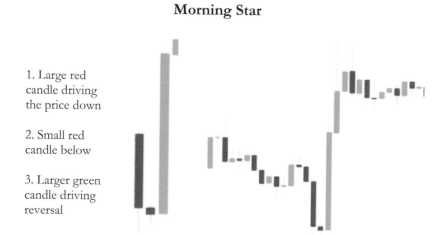

1. Large red candle driving the price down

2. Small red candle below

3. Larger green candle driving reversal

Figure 5.11 (tradingview charts)

The morning star is bullish reversal formation defined by a large red candle, a smaller red candle (often a doji or spinning top) situated *below* the first candle, and finishing with a large tall-bodied green candle. The green candle does not need to be larger than the first red candle; however, it should be a majority of the size. Also, if a small middle candle is situated inside the body of the first candle, then it is likely a harami and harami confirmation – not a morning star.

NOTE: Traditionally, traders often require that the morning star and its bearish counterpart, the evening star, have gaps between the middle candle and the two candles it's situated between. Thus, the middle candle in other markets may be red or green. Of course, we don't see this in the perpetual markets. So, look for a middle red candle opening downward from the first candle's close and the final green candle opening upward directly from the middle candle's close.

Tweezer Bottom

Figure 5.12 (tradingview chart)

The tweezer bottom is formed when, in a downtrend, two consecutive candles close with identical or nearly identical lows. Whether the candles are body or wick dominant doesn't matter as long as they share matching lows. Thus, it could be formed by two tall-bodied candles (see Figure 5.12) or by candle combinations with wicks. Tweezer bottoms show two successive periods where sellers failed to push the price further down, ending with buyers firmly in control. However, tweezer bottoms may be difficult to identify because candle sequences often end flat during periods of consolidation. Therefore, traders should carefully watch the next candle(s) for confirmation and to establish whether the pattern marks a break in trend.

Three White Soldiers

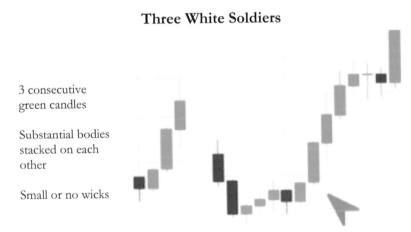

3 consecutive green candles

Substantial bodies stacked on each other

Small or no wicks

Figure 5.13 (tradingview charts)

The three white soldiers formation is defined by three consecutive well-bodied green candles stacking on top of each other, which appear in a downtrend or dip. Generally speaking, the candles will not have large wicks and have relatively tall bodies (no spinning tops or dojis). This formation shows consistent and strengthening buy pressure and often indicates a bullish reversal or increasing velocity of an existing bullish trend.

Three-Line Strike

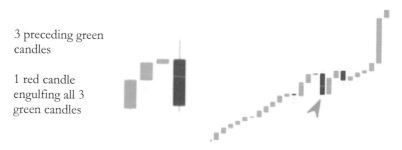

3 preceding green candles

1 red candle engulfing all 3 green candles

Figure 5.14 (tradingview charts)

A bullish three-line strike is formed during an uptrend when a single red candle eliminates the value of the previous three green candles before continuing the trend. While intuitively a single red candle engulfing three green candles may appear bearish, the concept is that such a quick move evaporates sell power and offers buyers a discount opportunity before the trend continues up. Still, I am hesitant to trade the three-line strike as a bullish continuation. Trading stock markets, Bulkowski notes a reversal rate is as high as 65%.[xiii] Whether a bullish three-line strike is a continuation, or bearish reversal, is up for debate. So, keep in mind this formation can play out either way. Exemplified below in Figure 5.15 is a three-line strike acting as a reversal.

Figure 5.15 (tradingview chart)
An example of a three-line strike reversal.

Bearish Candles and Formations

The following are bearish candles and formations, which frequently suggest a bearish reversal. Similar to some bullish candles, the color of the candle is not necessarily relevant to the bearish disposition. For instance, a green candle may offer a bearish outlook. However, some traders may treat red candles with a greater bearish bias because the candle closed below the open. Where relevant, I note where the color of the candle must be red.

Bearish Spinning Top

Figure 5.16 (tradingview charts)

The spinning top is a candle with both a substantial upper and lower wick as well as a short body. The body doesn't have to be perfectly centered; however, if it's situated on the top or bottom it may be another candle like a hammer or shooting star. Also, if the body looks more like the cross of a "t," then the candle is likely a doji, which is a relative of the spinning top. Spinning tops appear frequently and show indecision in the market and a period where buyers and sellers each held a dominating position before losing it. Spinning tops appear commonly in times of consolidation, continuation, and reversal. While they are not innately bullish or bearish leaning, a spinning top that occurs after a significant uptrend can mark a shift in the power struggle and indicate a bearish reversal. Remember, the color of the candle is determined by who controlled the price action at close of the time period and is not necessarily relevant to determining a bearish disposition. In other words, a green spinning top can be a bearish indicator at the end of an uptrend.

Shooting Star

Figure 5.17 (tradingview charts)

As you may notice, the shooting star is the bearish counterpart to the bullish hammer but it shares the same form as an inverted hammer (upside-down hammer). Like an inverted hammer, the candle has a long upper wick and a lowly placed body with little or no bottom wick. The candle shows buyers gaining the upper hand at some point before losing it, and the range between open and close is narrow. The difference between an inverted hammer and shooting star is where they occur. A bullish inverted hammer frequently occurs in a downtrend and indicates a weakening of selling power, while a bearish shooting star frequently occurs in an uptrend and indicates buyer exhaustion and a bearish reversal.

Hanging Man

Figure 5.18 (tradingview charts)

The hanging man is the bearish counterpart to the inverted hammer but it shares the same form as a bullish hammer. It's defined by its long lower wick, small upper body (head), and little or no top wick. The hanging man shows buyers losing control before gaining all or nearly all of it back. While this might not sound bearish intuitively because the bulls quickly recovered the period price after a drop; the hanging man shows the bears challenging the uptrend and an attempt at reversal. When appearing after a substantial uptrend, a hanging man may be a sell signal or simply a cautionary signal to the bulls hinting they may be losing steam.

Bearish Engulfing Candle

Figure 5.19 (tradingview charts)

A bearish engulfing candle is the opposite of a bullish engulfing candle. It occurs when the body of a larger, seller dominated, red candle follows a smaller-bodied, buyer dominated, green candle. Thus, the body of the red candle completely "engulfs" the preceding green candle without consideration to the wicks. This formation requires the red candle close below the previous green candle's open so the previous green candle is completely engulfed. It displays sellers recapturing control by completely overtaking and invalidating the previous period move.

NOTE: Traditionally, a stock trader may say the open of the red candle must be higher than the close of the green candle and gap up; however, as mentioned previously, our markets are 24/7 and do not gap like a stock market between trading hours. So, look for a candle opening at the same level and engulfing the previous candle.

Evening Star

Figure 5.20 (tradingview chart)

The evening star is the bearish version of the morning star. The formation consists of a large green candle, a small green candle *above* the first green candle (often a doji or spinning top), and then a large red candle comprising a majority of the first large green candle. Evening stars show a substantial push by the bulls followed by an inability to move the market higher and completes with a large bearish candle indicating sellers have firmly taken control. If the small middle candle is situated inside the body of the first candle, then it is likely a bearish harami and harami confirmation – not an evening star.

NOTE: Traditionally, traders often require that the evening star and its bullish counterpart, the morning star, have gaps between the middle candle and the two candles it's situated between. Thus, the middle candle in other markets may be red or green. Of course, we don't see this in the perpetual markets. So, look for a middle green candle opening upward from the first candle's close and the final red candle opening downward directly from the middle candle's close.

Bearish Harami

Large green candle

Smaller red candle inside the green one

Figure 5.21 (tradingview charts)

The bearish harami is defined by a larger exterior green candle with a smaller succeeding red candle inside. This is the bearish upside-down version of the "pregnant woman" candle formation. The belly candle is formed on top rather than the bottom. Bearish haramis display a pause in volatility and can indicate that trend reversal is imminent in an uptrend; however, bearish haramis that fail can result in a sharp rise. Thus, many traders wait for confirmation with an additional candle (the three inside down confirmation pattern).

NOTE: Traditionally, traders often require the belly candle of the harami to gap down inside the mother candle's body and some may give more weight to a harami when the belly candle's wicks are completely inside the mother candle's body. However, unless you are trading futures or an exchange that has time frame gaps, as noted in the previous section on time frames, you will not see such a strict definition of a bearish harami in crypto.

Bearish Harami Cross

Large green
outside candle

Inside doji or
thin spinning
top

Figure 5.22 (tradingview charts)

Similar to the bullish equivalent, a doji, or thin spinning top, inside a previous large green candlestick creates a bearish harami cross. If the small candle is situated above the larger green candle, it may be an evening star. Some traders may give greater weight to a bearish harami cross over a normal bearish harami as a reversal signal. As with all haramis, traders should watch for a further confirmation candle.

Three Inside Down (Bearish Harami Confirmation)

Large green
candle followed
by small red
inverted "belly"

Additional red
confirmation
candle

Harami "belly"

2nd red candle

Figure 5.23 (tradingview charts)

The three inside down pattern is a bearish confirmation pattern following the bearish harami. One additional red candle establishes seller control and confirms the preceding red candle (the inverted belly). This is a common short or sell signal for traders playing the harami.

Tweezer Top

Figure 5.24 (tradingview charts)

The tweezer top is formed when, in an uptrend, two consecutive candles close with identical or nearly identical highs creating a tweezer-like shape. Whether the candles are body or wick dominant doesn't matter as long as they share matching highs. Thus, it could be formed by two tall-bodied candles or by candle combinations with wicks. Tweezer tops show two successive periods where buyers failed to push the price further, ending with sellers firmly in control. However, tweezer tops may be difficult to identify because candle sequences often end flat during periods of consolidation. Hence, traders should carefully watch the next candle(s) for confirmation and to establish whether the pattern marks a trend break.

Three Black Crows

3 consecutive red candles

Substantial bodies stacked on each other

Small or no wicks

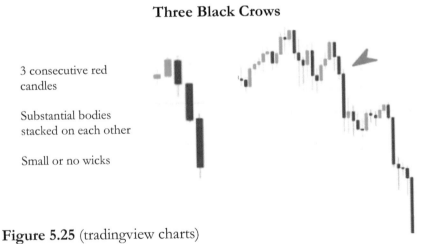

Figure 5.25 (tradingview charts)

The three black crows formation is the bearish version of the three white soldiers and is defined by three consecutive well-bodied red candles.

Generally speaking, the candles will not have large wicks and have relatively tall bodies (no spinning tops or dojis). This formation shows consistent and strengthening sell pressure and often indicates a bearish reversal or increasing velocity of an existing bearish trend.

Bearish Three-Line Strike

Figure **5.26** (tradingview charts)

A bearish three-line strike is formed when a single green candle recovers the value of the previous three red candles. While intuitively this may appear bullish, the concept is that such a quick move evaporates buy power and offers an opportunity for sellers to unload quickly at a higher point before the trend continues down. Similar to the bullish three-line strike, whether a bearish three-line strike is a bearish continuation or bullish reversal is up for debate. So, keep in mind this pattern can play out either way.

Dojis

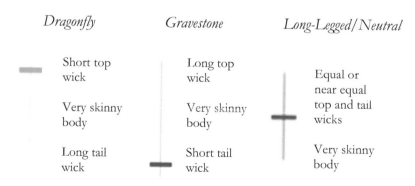

Figure **5.27** (tradingview excerpts)

Highlighted in this illustration are the common types of dojis.

The doji is a trader favorite for chart interpretation, particularly when marking potential trend reversals. Doji's signal indecision in the market and can be bullish, bearish, or neutral. Doji's always represent a power struggle where one side had control but lost it. In the case of a long-legged or neutral doji, both sides had control at one point before losing it and ending in a stalemate.

A doji is similar to the spinning top or hammer form candles. Notably, the difference between them is the height of the body. If a body is fuller than what would fit as the cross of a "t," then it's a different candle, such as a spinning top, hammer, or shooting star. Importantly, even if you can't quite tell whether a candle is a doji, spinning top, hammer, or shooting star - long wicks in general are indicative of the opposing side's inability to further move the asset price and are often an opportunity for a trader to see weakness in a trend. In other words, recognizing the bigger picture of what the wick means can help you make a determination even if you are not correctly identifying the candle.

Dragonfly Doji

Figure 5.28 (tradingview chart)

The dragonfly doji is a bull's best friend. Distinguished by its long bottom wick and cross shape, it displays an attempt by sellers to push the price of an asset down significantly before bulls recover a vast majority or all of value in that period. The close of the candle is extremely close to the open. When appearing after a sustained downtrend, a dragonfly doji can signal a bottom. In these cases, it often shows the last gasp of sell pressure before tides turn. The candle itself can be either red or green without changing its bullish disposition. If a candle's body is greater than what fits comfortably as the cross of a "t," it may be a spinning top, bullish hammer, or hanging man depending on its appearance or location. Importantly, despite its bullish bias, a dragonfly doji can appear the top of an uptrend and signify a reversal – similar to a hanging man.

Gravestone Doji

Figure 5.29 (tradingview chart)

The gravestone doji is the opposite of a dragonfly doji. As such, it's a bear's best friend. Inverse to a dragonfly doji, a gravestone doji is marked by its long top wick and skinny body that forms with a close nearly at the candle's open. The candle itself can be either red or green without changing its bearish disposition. This doji is formed when buyers push the price of an asset up significantly before giving it all back. When occurring after a sustained bull trend, it can signal the final bullish gasp and indicate the top. If a candle looks like a gravestone doji, but the body is greater than what fits comfortably as the cross of a "t," it could be a spinning top, inverted hammer, or shooting star depending on the body's placement and where the candle appears. Importantly, despite its bearish bias, a gravestone doji can appear at the bottom of an uptrend and signify a reversal – similar to an inverted hammer.

Long-Legged/ Neutral Dojis

Figure 5.30 (tradingview chart)

The long-legged doji and the neutral doji are basically the same thing except the neutral or "classic" doji has shorter wicks. Both can signal a top, bottom, or consolidation. These dojis are notably different from the other dojis by the distinct small body situated in the middle (or middle-ish area) of the candle rather than near the top or bottom. Long-legged and neutral dojis show a tug of war that resulted in a virtual draw. At one point, both the buyers and sellers each had control but when the time period closed, neither side had a clear advantage. Like other dojis, the candle body is almost non-existent as the open and close were nearly the same.

Despite not having an innate bearish or bullish bias, the long-legged or neutral dojis can certainly be interpreted with a bias. For example, if one appears after a sustained trend in either direction it may signal the inability of the prevailing force to push the price further in that direction and mark a reversal. When appearing after a sustained bullish trend, it may signal a top. Conversely, when appearing after a sustained bearish trend, it may signal a bottom. However, a long-legged or neutral doji may also appear at times of consolidation because they show indecision in the market and the inability of both buyers and sellers to take the upper hand. Thus, when confronting these dojis, a trader needs to pay special attention to the surrounding circumstances.

Candlestick Takeaways:

1. Candles are formed by price action over an examined period of time and contain wicks and bodies.

2. Candlestick formations show the power struggle between buyers and sellers and are frequently used for timing reversals.

3. Bullish or bearish candlesticks are not always green and red, respectively.

4. Similar looking candlesticks may signal different things depending on their location and the current trend.

5. Candlesticks should be read in light of other aspects of technical analysis and the chart as a whole.

CHAPTER 6:
TREND LINES

Learning Japanese candlesticks is only one small part of a much greater equation. While individual candles and candlestick formations can give predictive hints about what is to come next, when read in conjunction with the greater price action, the predictive ability strengthens. As candlesticks string together, ebbing and flowing with the price action, highs and lows are created. Traders can analyze these highs and lows using trend lines and can further predict future market movements when these trend lines break or create recurring chart patterns. These next sections focus on trend line formation, breakouts and breakdowns, and trend channels.

Basic Trend Line Tool for Chart Construction

Figure 6.1
(tradingview excerpt)

The most fundamental and useful tool for charting is the trend line. To draw a trend line on a Tradingview chart, select the second tool down on the left toolbar next to the asset name.

The trend line simply draws a line from two points and you can use it to demark all support and resistance lines, which are the basis of chart patterns. The following sections define these in detail.

Also, other lines like rays exist, which can be used for flat tops or bottoms and price points you think may act as support or resistance.

Trend Line Formation

As an asset's price rises and falls it creates a continuous series of highs and lows. A high being the highest price of the asset before sellers take control and drive the price down, and a low being the lowest price of the asset before buyers take control and drive the price back up again. When a new low or new high is created, a trader may analyze the new high or low relative to the previous highs or lows. Often, successive highs or lows follow a general trend of price action and can be connected using a line to create what is called a trend line. Trend lines connect the lows to the lows and the highs to the highs. They follow the overall movement of the market – either an uptrend, downtrend, or consolidation. An uptrend is formed in periods of higher highs and higher lows, while a downtrend is formed in periods of lower highs and lower lows. A period of consolidation may be defined by a largely horizontal period with a narrow range of highs and lows.

Generally, at least three successive highs or lows (touches on the same line) create a trend line. As a rule of thumb, the more touches on a particular trend line the more significant it will be if it's breached. However, in some instances, you can draw a potential trend line from two highs or lows and see how it fills in understanding it may not be very accurate. I find two-touch lines occasionally useful when connecting consecutive highs or lows on very large time frames like 1D or 1W to see greater trend direction and predict future macro highs or lows.

Whether to draw the trend line by attaching the points of the candle wicks or the bodies is a matter of preference. Some traders have a hard preference and only stick to wicks or bodies, while other traders create trend lines using both - maximizing connections that can be made to a particular line. I prefer to give wicks first preference because they pinpoint the exact price points. Yet, bodies often make more connections and average the trend range nicely. Ultimately, a trend line is merely delineating the upper or lower limit of trending price action, and I see no problem doing it either way. Moreover, sometimes a trend line may have a slight deviation and recovery before continuing to maintain the trend. Thus, an unremarkable deviation. However, a significant and sustained breach of a trend line should be obvious regardless of whether it was drawn using wicks, bodies, or both.

Wicks   **Bodies**

Figure 6.2 (tradingview charts)
An example of drawing the same trend line using wicks for one instance and bodies for the other. Notice how a relatively small rise would break beyond both trend line examples regardless of how they were drawn.

Support and Resistance Lines

A trend line connecting a series of lows (higher lows or lower lows) creates what is called a support line (see Figure 6.3). Conversely, a trend line connecting a series of highs (higher highs or lower highs) creates what is called a resistance line (see Figure 6.3). The resistance line delineates the upper trend of price action and establishes where the buyers are repeatedly unable to push the price above. Similarly, the support line delineates the lower trend of price action and establishes where the sellers are repeatedly unable to push the price below.

Figure 6.3 Support and Resistance Lines (tradingview charts)

Breakouts and Breakdowns

A breakout occurs when buyers push the price of an asset above the resistance line. This shows the buyers thrusting the price beyond the general trend of price action, which suggests a shift in trend or a volatile move. For instance, in a downtrend with three or more consecutive highs, each lower than the last, buyers force a breakout disrupting the trend of lower highs. This suggests the downtrend may be broken and a positive reversal is imminent. In an uptrend or consolidation period, if a resistance line is breached it may signal a new accelerating move upward.

Figure 6.4 (tradingview chart)
Highlighted above is a resistance line and breakout. Notice the unremarkable single deviation right before touch three of the resistance line. The X marks the breakout.

A breakdown occurs when sellers push the price of an asset below the support line. This shows sellers pushing the price below the general trend of price action and also suggests a shift in trend. For example, in an uptrend with three or more consecutive higher lows, the sellers push the price below the third higher low, which breaks below the support line. This suggests the uptrend supported by higher lows is broken and a reversal may be occurring. Additionally, in a downtrend or consolidation period, if a support line is breached it may mark a new accelerating downward move of the asset. Importantly, I use the term breakdown in this handbook because it's easy to differentiate support and resistance breaks. Breakouts always being upward moves and breakdowns being downward. Many traders will use the term breakout interchangeably for both cases. That is not the case for this handbook.

Figure 6.5 (tradingview chart)
Notice the support line is drawn using the most consecutive connecting wicks possible, and thus the first arrow marks an outlier. Also note, the second arrow marks a near touch but not quite. X marks the breakdown.

Breakouts and breakdowns are often an opportunity for a trader and indicate an entry or exit. In the case of a breakout, a trader may buy or long an asset hoping to get an entry at the first indication of positive trend reversal or bullish continuation. Conversely, upon breakdown, a trader may sell a position to preserve profit or enter a short and profit from the first indication of negative trend reversal or a continuation downward. Frequently upon initial breakout or breakdown, assets revisit ("retest") the point of the breakout, which some traders use as an entry point. This is particularly true with chart pattern breaks, which are discussed thoroughly in subsequent sections.

Finally, a broken resistance line can turn into a support line and vice versa. Sometimes when an asset breaks a resistance or support line, and the price returns to the trend line, what once was resistance may then act as support. A trader may say something like "resistance has flipped to support" or "support has flipped to resistance." This trend line switch may be observed shortly after the initial breakout or days, weeks, or even months later. If a trend line was respected for many weeks or months before breaking, traders may place greater significance on the line if price action reverses course and approaches or retests it.

Figure 6.6 (tradingview chart)
See this resistance line (bodies) now acting as support after a breakout and retest.

Fakeouts

A fakeout refers to a false breakout or breakdown where the resistance or support line is briefly breached before the asset reverses back below or above the trend line. Fakeouts are the misery of the breakout trader. In some instances, fakeouts result in a strong rejection and can lead to a powerful move in the opposite direction. For example, if a breakout occurs and rejects the higher high, short sellers may pile in and quickly drive the asset's price down. Or, in the opposite situation, if a breakdown occurs and fails quickly bouncing back above the support line, buyers may jump in and quickly drive the price higher. Fakeouts can develop quickly and be comprised of a single candle or they may develop over a short period of time following a trend break and encompass a group of succeeding candles. Generally, fakeouts indicate weakening power on the side that failed to sustain the price beyond the trend line. You may hear traders say the term "bear trap" or "bull trap," which means an instance where over eager bears or bulls are fooled into taking a bad position. This saying is frequently applied to fakeouts.

Figure 6.7 VET/BTC, 1D, 2020, Binance (tradingview chart)
In this example, notice how the resistance line was broken before a quick rejection and return back below the line. Ultimately, however, this falling wedge pattern broke out massively.

Trend Channels

A trend channel is formed when an asset's price ranges between parallel support and resistance lines for a substantial period of time. Generally, there should be at least three touches for each line. Since trend lines run parallel to each other, the channel either moves in an upward direction with higher highs on the resistance line and higher lows on the support line or downward with lower highs on the resistance line and lower lows on the support line. Trend channels are traded upon an asset breaking out or below the resistance or support line. The breakout or breakdown suggests the asset is ready to leave the narrow range of the channel and continue a move in the direction of the break.

See the example below, charting the entire altcoin market capitalization (excluding Bitcoin), which I use as an index for the health of the altcoin market (Ticker: TOTAL2). If a trader used the trend channel breaks as buy signals and went into any major altcoin, both occasions would have netted a healthy profit since the altcoin market capitalization rose 180% and 95% respectively. Notably, larger altcoins harbor a significant portion of the market share.

Figure 6.8 (tradingview chart)
Total Altcoin Market Capitalization Excluding BTC (Ticker: TOTAL2)

Trend Line Takeaways:

1. Trend lines are created by connecting highs to highs (resistance) and lows to lows (support).

2. Generally, the more touches on a line, the bigger the implication of a break.

3. A breakout occurs when the resistance line is broken, while a breakdown occurs when the support line is broken.

4. A fakeout refers to a failed breakout or breakdown.

5. Trend channels are formed by two parallel, non-converging trend lines.

CHAPTER 7:
CHART PATTERNS

Trend support and resistance lines are also the basis of chart pattern formation. By applying the basics of trend lines and combining both support and resistance lines, traders identify patterns that can be used as predictive tools. Interestingly, numerous repeatedly identifiable patterns occur in all markets, which allow traders to predict future movements of price action with reasonable success. Over the years, traders have applied the statistical significance of price action following frequently occurring chart patterns and their relevance to which way a market moves.[xiv] Today, Chart Logic offers the first comprehensive analysis of chart patterns in the cryptocurrency markets. This chapter first describes when to enter and exit a breakout trade before showing individual examples of some of the most commonly known chart patterns, their application in crypto markets, and detailed statistics and findings on each pattern's performance.

When to Enter a Breakout Trade

When targeting any breakout, a trader should ensure the trend is actually broken. Traders are cautioned not to long at or just below a resistance line or short at or just above a support line. While it may be temping because a breakout or breakdown is so close you can taste it, trend lines tend to support the direction of price action they define and should be presumed to be maintained until broken. In fact, many traders like to place bids at support lines and sells or shorts at resistance lines.

Whether to buy upon trend line break or candle completion is another question. Many traders believe you should only buy a breakout that confirms with at least one completed candle (after the candle closes beyond the broken trend line). However, other traders will buy a breakout upon the trend breaking because, on some occasions, a breakout occurs so violently and quickly that a trader would be left in the dust if they waited for candle completion. Other traders will wait for a retrace or retest following a breakout that goes back to the original trend line. This is a preference subject to personal taste.

Each of these strategies comes with a downside. Arguably, breakout traders that do not wait for any confirmation are playing the riskiest game, particularly those traders who are using leverage to trade, because many breakouts fail. However, that risk may be worth taking if an extremely violent breakout is reasonably anticipated. Retest traders rely on the fact that often breakouts retest the trend line; however, on many occasions breakouts never retest the trend line and leave these traders to buy in higher or not at all. Logically, I've never been attracted to retest trading because of the risk of missing a move and the fact that retest traders still buy at the trend line near breakout and must set a stop-loss below anyways, which accomplishes little more than what a breakout trader does with a fine-tuned stop-limit order. However, if you miss an initial breakout, I see a retest as an opportunity for a second chance entry. Finally, traders who wait for one or more candle to complete may miss out on some explosive trades or get a higher entry, but they do not assume the high risk of common fakeouts and they still may reap the benefit of a retest if it occurs. Thus, for general purposes, as a new trader I suggest taking the road of a confirmation trader.

When to Exit a Failed Breakout Trade

Determining a proper exit can be a challenge. However, if you are not over leveraged, allowing some latitude gives a trader a comfortable edge on volatility. Numerous popular chart pattern examples offered online show the buy signal for a breakout as above the resistance line and a stop-loss signal just below the support line of the same pattern (for short setups – vice versa). In many instances, this can be an acceptable strategy. The logic is that if the price reverses to the point where the pattern breaks down, it's no longer valid. This strategy is particularly effective when the pattern is one where support and resistance lines converge creating a narrow price range at the time of breakout or breakdown. For instance, with many pennants, triangles, and flags. However, in some cases like broadening wedges, the price difference between the support and resistance lines may be too significant to place a reasonable stop-loss beyond the opposing trend line.

Other factors may also play into where you decide to exit, like position sizing and acceptable losses. Before you enter a trade, you should pre-determine how much money you are willing to lose and make a hard rule on when to cut your losses. When I am stopped out of a trade, I do not seek to re-enter that day because doing so is an easy way to succumb to gamblers' mentality. Please carefully read the sections on adopting hard rules and gamblers' mentality in Part III of this handbook.

Ultimately, the decision of what is an acceptable loss and placement for your stop-loss is a judgment call. A trader will learn quickly that it's one thing to say how they would trade a chart from the sidelines, but when they are actually in the trade with their capital on the line, it may feel completely different. This is precisely why all trades should have a predetermined entry and exit (stop-loss) and trade strategies should be executed from an objective and robotic standpoint. There will always be another trade.

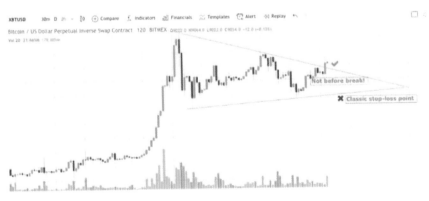

Figure 7.1 BTC/XBT, 2H, 2020, Bitmex (tradingview chart)
Check out this classic example of an entry and potential exit based on a confirmed breakout of a pennant pattern (2H). The breakout is confirmed above the resistance line. The stop-loss is set below the support line.

Taking Profit

Every trade should come with some idea of when ideally you will be taking profit – either abstractly or definitively. Many traders mark profit points before they even enter the trade. These may be based on considerations like resistance lines; price levels; levels based on pattern formation and statistical performance; former price points where a significant amount of volume occurred; or through technical indicators like Fibonacci lines or moving averages. Securing profit can be done all at once by exiting an entire position or a trader may take profit along the way as a winner rides a trend. Stop-losses should be moved when a position is profitable to secure gains.

As you will see, however, I specifically do not delineate hard (definitive) profit points on chart patterns or trends highlighted for this handbook and do not frequently follow a strict system where "if X crypto breaks out it will reach Y target level." Why? Because frankly profit points are often arbitrary and may vary significantly depending on the particular disposition of each chart. Thus, assuming each pattern or trend break will result in a specific target seems futile.

What I look for, rather, are technical indicators signaling a weakening in the move or a looming reversal and make each determination on a case-by-case basis. In other words, *I look to take profit and exit a trade on the same grounds and for the same reason I entered the trade: the technical disposition of the chart suggests an imminent reversal.* In conjunction, I look to past pattern performance for guidance, but it depends dominantly on whether technical indicators are present.

This is not to say traders who highlight specific targets are going to be wrong or that I don't do it on occasion. Merely, I am saying I don't believe black and white profit points always exist for each trade, especially before it begins. So, I don't want to leave an unrealistic impression on new traders. I look to maximize returns in a dynamic market based on what the technical indicators suggest as it evolves. Nevertheless, when I have a position that is comfortably in the profit zone, I rearrange stop-losses to ensure the position will remain profitable. If you feel more comfortable trading with specific targets and apply any of the methodologies mentioned in the paragraphs above, I see no problem with that. In Chapter 10 of Part III, I teach my evidence-based approach to tackling each trade and offer an example trade going through the entire process, including profit taking. Please refer to this section to see a profit-taking illustration in action. The Divergences in Action section in Chapter 8 also exhibits a nice profit-taking illustration.

Chart Pattern Performance Analysis and Methodology

This analysis aims to help traders better understand the performance of commonly occurring chart patterns in the volatile cryptocurrency markets. To date, no crypto-centric statistics exist for traders to gauge past performance of chart patterns. To assist the crypto community with this endeavor, I examined the top 100 cryptocurrencies (excluding stable coins and a few coins with insufficient data or other flaws) to draw statistics on each commonly occurring pattern. For each pattern, I derived the frequencies of breakouts vs. breakdowns, trend continuations vs. reversals, and I measured the gain or decline percentage between a breakout or breakdown and the next relative period of consolidation or trend reversal. Traders can use breakout direction and averaged price performance findings as tools when considering future pattern-based trades. Moreover, trend continuation and reversal frequencies may be particularly useful when examining patterns with a specific preceding trend bias or if the breakout statistics are near a 50-50 coin toss.

For each crypto, both the charts for USD(T) traded pairs and Bitcoin (BTC) traded pairs were examined. Thereby ensuring traders see any differences in market behavior between both types of commonly traded markets. I also provide the combined averages exclusively for handbook readers interested in the aggregate data. However, in several instances, the results clearly indicate differences between USD(T) and BTC traded pairs. Therefore, I suggest traders pay particular attention to the performance for each individually traded pair because the findings are going to be more precise for the market you are trading.

All statistics are derived from only the 1D charts. Consequently, these statistics are only relevant to daily time frame chart pattern performance and are geared toward swing and position traders. I strongly urge new traders to only trade chart patterns on larger time frames (1D or 4H). While identifiable patterns occur on very short frames, including down to the 1-minute chart, the reliability of the patterns in my opinion is greatly reduced. Of course, the gain or decline percentages will also generally be much smaller on shorter time frames.

The study examined chart pattern performance on the basis of relativity. Meaning, the gain or decline was measured by the distance between the breakout/breakdown and the high or low at the next trend reversal or period of consolidation relative to the examined pattern's size. Considerations included the duration and size of the next succeeding consolidation period, the initial run up of the examined pattern (i.e. pole length), and any trend break following the initial pattern. If the following period(s) of consolidation was smaller than the initial pattern, then two or more consecutive periods could be counted until the relative size of the initial pattern was met. Figure 7.2 featured below highlights colored dashes marking the close points for the previous pattern(s). For hundreds of additional examples please see chartlogic.io.

Figure 7.2 NEO/BTC, 1D, 2016-2018, Bittrex (tradingview chart)

The measured gains are offered in three tiers: unfiltered averages, filtered averages excluding outliers over 400%, and filtered averages excluding any gainers over 100%. This is to give traders a multi-level means of measuring past performance. One of the obvious findings is crypto's overall superior price performance compared to equities or other markets. Understand, crypto is known for its extreme volatility, which is why it can be so lucrative to trade. Thus, don't simply assume averages negating all gainers over 100% are going to be the best gauge of future performance. In some cases, like descending triangles, a majority of those that broke out positively well out-performed a 100% gain. So, consider the possible significance of each tier. Tiers may be tested as targets, and, in a future edition, I will convey results for tier-based targets.

Chart patterns were broken down into two primary categories: continuation-biased patterns and top and bottom reversal patterns. Each continuation-biased pattern was examined for its tendency to breakout or breakdown as a whole, irrespective of any preceding trend disposition. Additionally, patterns were also examined for continuation performance based on breakouts and breakdowns following an *immediately preceding* uptrend (bull trend) or downtrend (bear trend). A "C" or "R" designation for each examined pattern distinguished whether the pattern continued or reversed its immediately preceding trend (the trend intact when the pattern began – relative to the examined pattern's size).

Please note, volume is omitted on initial pattern identification examples in this handbook to provide the clearest examples of form. As with all trading methods described in this handbook, each pattern should be analyzed in light of the totality of the circumstances and in conjunction with other indicators and techniques.

Finally, understand the data came solely from the top 100 cryptos and their limited historical record. I did my best to source charts that spanned the entire history of each crypto. Some went back as far as 2015 or earlier, while many others are newer and came around during or after the 2017 ICO boom. Consequently, the limited historical record of crypto means limited data for pattern analysis. In total, roughly 1,800 patterns were carefully examined manually under a rigid set of rules. For a complete summary of the methodology, see the end of the book or read chartlogic.io/methodology.

Many common continuations patterns and some reversal patterns were adequately represented in the data for analysis, however, some patterns, particularly rare types of bottoms only had a few examples. Still, I define and give examples and data for them. I try to note all cases where I think data is insufficient or should be taken lightly but readers should judge for themselves how they want to interpret the sample sizes and findings. Also, some tables have an asterisk noting where findings may be unbalanced and should be taken lightly. Overall, understand the limitations of the study and know that more data will be added over time and these numbers may change as more data is aggregated. Nevertheless, the findings are very interesting and some have already affected how I trade, and I am excited to share them with you!

Note: The patterns described and defined in this handbook follow the definitions I use and apply in the crypto markets and may not coincide precisely with definitions of the same patterns used by other traders for trading stocks, commodities, or other commonly traded assets. The pattern definition and recognition here is to give traders the best examples of chart patterns in the crypto markets. Many other patterns and other definitions exist, and I encourage readers to use this as a stepping-stone to explore the wider world of pattern analysis. In terms of pattern durations, I try to stay consistent with widely used stock traders, but some things may differ.

Continuation-Biased Patterns

Continuation patterns are exactly as they sound – they tend to continue the trend that already exists. For example, if the current trend is bearish with lower highs and lower lows, a continuation pattern is likely to complete with a downside break that furthers the bearish trend. Similarly, if the current trend is bullish with higher highs and higher lows, a continuation pattern is likely to further the bullish trend with an upside break. Continuation patterns can offer traders a fresh entry into an existing trend or affirm a bias and justify keeping an existing position in the current trend. Importantly, continuation patterns have a bias, but they may break the other way signaling a temporary or enduring reversal. So, it's important to understand when traders say continuation pattern that they mean a pattern more commonly associated with a continuation than reversal.

Flags

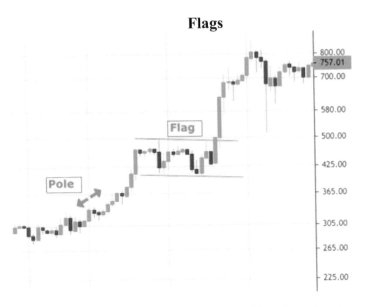

Figure 7.3 ETH/USD, 1D, 2019, Kraken (tradingview chart)

The flag is a classic short-term and continuation-biased pattern. Marked by its long run-up or downtrend (the pole) followed by a rectangular or parallelogram consolidation (the flag). A flag is different from a pennant in that a flag is rectangular or shaped like a parallelogram. However, both have the pole preceding the consolidation period. Additionally, flags may point downward or upward like a wedge, however, a wedge has two converging or fanning trend lines rather than parallel trend lines. If the consolidation is triangular, then it's not a flag but a triangle, pennant, or wedge depending on the shape and duration of formation. For the purpose of this study, all rectangular or parallelogram flags, regardless of duration and angle, were considered. All flags must have at least two touches on each trend line (support and resistance).

Bull Flags

Figure 7.4 XMR/USDT, 1D, May 2019, Binance (tradingview chart)

A bull flag is marked by a rectangular or parallelogram consolidation (flag) following a steep bullish run-up (pole). The bull flag demonstrates bullish consolidation during an uptrend and upon breakout often continues the trend. The flag portion marks a brief pause in the buyers' overall excitement and a controlled retracement before an asset's price rise continues. For traders who enjoy pattern targets, another pole's length is standard here.

Bear Flags

Figure 7.5 LTC/USD, 1D, 2018, Coinbase (tradingview chart)

The bear flag is the opposite of a bull flag and is marked by its inverted flagpole, temporary rectangular or parallelogram consolidation, and continuation downward. The flag marks a brief pause in the sellers' overall enthusiasm before an asset's decline continues. Support break marks the entry. Similar to the bullish counterpart, traders often target a pole's length below.

Table 7.1

Performance Statistics of Flags

	USD(T) Traded Pairs	BTC Traded Pairs	Combined Avgs.
# of Examined Patterns	211	196	407
Upside Breakout %	51.18%	39.8%	45.49%
Downside Breakdown %	48.82%	60.2%	54.51%
Trend Continuation % for Bull Flags (Preceding Bullish Trend)	84.61%	88.15%	86.38%
Trend Reversal % for Bull Flags (Preceding Bullish Trend)	15.39%	11.85%	13.62%
Trend Continuation % for Bear Flags (Preceding Bearish Trend)	90.42%	90.83%	90.62%
Trend Reversal % for Bear Flags (Preceding Bearish Trend)	9.58%	9.17%	9.37%
Unfiltered Avg. % Gain from Upside Breakout	169.88%	86.37%	128.12%
Avg. % Decline from Downside Breakdown	-46.71%	-37.05%	-41.88%

Filtered Avg. % Gain from Upside Breakout (Excluding Outliers Over 400%)	89.12%	76.21%	82.66%
Filtered Avg. % Gain from Upside Breakout (Excluding Gainers Over 100%)	50.17%	46.74%	48.45%

Summary of the Findings

According to this study, flags live up to their continuation reputation. Despite results indicating a slight overall bearish bias visible in the total breakout vs. breakdown ratios at 45.49% vs. 54.51%, the consistency of flags acting as continuation patterns is irrefutable. Bull flags found in USD(T) pairs continued the trend 84.61% of the time, while bear flags continued downward 90.42% of the time. BTC pairs showed similar results with bull flags continuing the trend upward 88.15% of the time, while bear flags continued downward 90.83% of the time.

Notably, price performance leaned heavily to USD(T) pairs with unfiltered gains roughly twice as high as those in the BTC pairs. The breakdown performance also weighed heavily toward USD(T) traded pairs with an average decline of -46.71% vs BTC pairs' -37.05%. So, traders using USD(T) pairs may reasonably expect greater volatility when trading flags. The elevated volatility of USD(T) pairs is a common theme with nearly all patterns and is noted in this section and also addressed in greater detail in Chapter 11 of Part III. Interestingly, bull flags also appeared more frequently in USD(T) pairs, while bear flags appeared more frequently in BTC pairs, which may help explain why BTC pairs show a heavier overall bearish disposition with 60.2% breaking down. For more on this insight, please also read Chapter 11.

Pennants

Figure 7.6 LTC/USD, 1D, 2019, Coinbase (tradingview chart)

A pennant is another common short-term continuation-biased pattern marked by its pole and triangular or wedgy consolidation. The key difference between a pennant and a triangle or wedge is the duration of formation. Triangles and wedges are formed over longer periods (21 or more days), while pennants are formed over shorter periods (several days to 20 days). Structurally, however, they may look similar. Because of the short duration in which pennants are formed, I tend to only seek a minimum two touches on each support and resistance line so long as the consolidation is tightly triangular or wedgy. Like flags, many traders target a pole's length.

Notably, a day trader or scalp trader may not care for the time-based pennant distinction and may call low-frame patterns by their triangular or wedge shape regardless of formation duration. One could also apply trading periods rather than days to distinguish triangles from pennants. For example, requiring pennants be formed under 21 periods (not necessarily 1D periods). However, the performance analysis results here would not be relevant.

Bull Pennants

Figure 7.7 (tradingview charts)
BNB/BTC, 1D, Dec. 2017, Binance (left); XMR/USD, 1D, Aug. 2017, Kraken (right)

Bull pennants form in a steep uptrend (the pole) and often signal upward continuation after a brief tick of triangular or wedgy consolidation. A break above the resistance line marks the entry.

Bear Pennants

Figure 7.8 (tradingview charts)
ADA/USD, 1D, July 2019, Kraken (left); BAT/BTC, 1D, June 2019, Bittrex (right)

The bear pennant is the opposite of the bull pennant and often signals a bearish continuation after a brief tick of consolidation. Bear pennants are marked by a declining flagpole and a triangular or wedgy consolidation. A break below the support line marks the entry.

Table 7.2

Performance Statistics of Pennants

	USD(T) Traded Pairs	BTC Traded Pairs	Combined Avgs.
# of Examined Patterns	358	324	682
Upside Breakout %	47.76%	44.75%	46.25%
Downside Breakdown %	52.24%	55.25%	53.74%
Trend Continuation % for Bull Pennants (Preceding Bullish Trend)	71.84%	68.88%	70.36%
Trend Reversal % for Bull Pennants (Preceding Bullish Trend)	28.16%	31.12%	29.64%
Trend Continuation % for Bear Pennants (Preceding Bearish Trend)	85.43%	85.41%	85.42%
Trend Reversal % for Bear Pennants (Preceding Bearish Trend)	14.57%	14.59%	14.58%
Unfiltered Avg. % Gain from Upside Breakout	140.66%	99.93%	120.29%
Avg. % Decline from Downside Breakdown	-39.9%	-30.6%	-35.25%
Filtered Avg. % Gain from Upside Breakout (Excluding Outliers Over 400%)	103.24%	78.87%	91.05%
Filtered Avg. % Gain from Upside Breakout	46.83%	50.6%	48.71%

Summary of the Findings

Pennants clearly support the continuation-biased theory in the crypto markets. While they broke upward and downward at a near equal rate on all charts individually and collectively, with a slight bearish bias for both pairs (53.74% total avg.), they tend to continue the immediately preceding trend a strong majority of the time. Of the USD(T) pairs, 71.84% of bull pennants continued the trend, while 85.43% of the bear pennants broke downward. Similarly, 68.88% of the bull pennants broke upward, while 85.41% of the bear pennants broke downward for BTC traded pairs. Undeniably, these findings show a strong correlation between pennants and trend continuation for both the USD(T) and BTC paired markets. Indeed, both markets shared strikingly similar results. These odds suggest pennants are a great pattern for a quick and lucrative continuation play.

Pennant price performance exhibited gains and declines in the moderate range for crypto. Breakdowns for both pairs were in the 30% range with USD(T) pairs breaking down further at 39.9%. Unfiltered gains were relatively modest with USD(T) pairs again showing increased volatility at 140.66% vs. BTC pairs' 99.93%. Imagine telling a stock trader a 100-140% average gain is modest! Interestingly, some of the largest gainers sampled in this study were from pennants like Matic/USD(T) with a 1,200% gainer, but the small movers appear to average those outliers nicely.

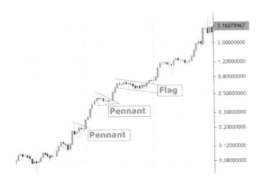

Figure 7.9
(tradingview chart)

STRAT/USD c., 1D, 2017, Bittrex

I chose this example sequence because it highlights realistic imperfections: 1) the 2nd pennant break consolidated again before moving a full pole's length, and 2) consolidation above the flag did not fit squarely in the box of a chart pattern but steered another continuation.

Triangles

Triangles, as a pattern class, are comprised of various triangular and continuation-biased patterns. Triangles are categorized by the slopes of the support and resistance lines and include symmetrical, ascending, and descending triangles. Triangles can be a bullish or bearish and a continuation or reversal pattern; however, different triangles support different biases. All triangles must be formed over at least 21 days and collectively have at least 5 touches on the support and resistance lines.

Symmetrical Triangles

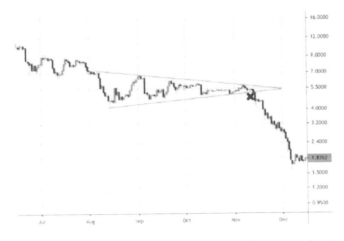

Figure 7.10 EOS/USD, 1D, 2018, Kraken (tradingview chart)

The symmetrical triangle is as it sounds – a triangle with symmetrical support and resistance lines (lower highs and higher lows). Symmetrical triangles can be continuation or reversal indicators, but, as detailed in the study below, they are dominantly bearish in the crypto markets. In Figure 7.10 above, the symmetrical triangle marked a bearish continuation. The difference between the symmetrical triangle and symmetrical-triangle-shaped pennant is the duration in which they are formed. Triangles form over weeks or months (21+ days), while pennants are a short-term consolidation. Thus, some shorter frame traders might even trade the lower highs and higher lows of symmetrical triangles as they form.

Figure 7.11
(tradingview chart)

Waves/BTC, 1W, 2017/18, Bittrex

An example of an "imperfect" pattern with the second lower high just short of the resistance line and touch 3 on the support is a little long. Still, I would not deny this pattern by being petty.

Featured above in Figure 7.11 is a multi-month symmetrical triangle from the WAVES/BTC weekly (1W) chart. Notice how the converging highs and lows created large valleys and consider how a swing trader could have capitalized using a trend channel for the second valley.

Table 7.3

Performance Statistics of Symmetrical Triangles

	USD(T) Traded Pairs	BTC Traded Pairs	Combined Avgs.
# of Examined Patterns	132	121	253
Upside Breakout %	37.88%	21.48%	29.68%
Downside Breakdown %	62.12%	78.52%	70.32%
Bullish Trend Continuation %	52.72%	23.4%	38.06%

(Preceding Bullish Trend)			
Trend Reversal % (Preceding Bullish Trend)	47.28%	76.6%	61.94%
Bearish Trend Continuation % (Preceding Bearish Trend)	74.64%	78.87%	76.75%
Trend Reversal % (Preceding Bearish Trend)	25.36%	21.13%	23.24%
Unfiltered Avg. % Gain from Upside Breakout	193.19%	142.05%	167.62%
Avg. % Decline from Downside Breakdown	-47.44%	-44.06%	-45.75%
Filtered Avg. % Gain from Upside Breakout (Excluding Outliers Over 400%)	104.29%	73.75%	89.02%
Filtered Avg. % Gain from Upside Breakout (Excluding Gainers Over 100%)	54.06%	51.15%	52.6%

Summary of the Findings

Contrary to what Bulkowski found in his widely used pattern analysis in the stock markets,[xv] symmetrical triangles do not support a bullish breakout bias in the crypto markets according to this study! In fact, they're overwhelmingly bearish on both USD(T) and BTC traded pairs. Overall, 70.32% of all symmetrical triangles broke downward. BTC traded pairs showed a striking 78.52% breakdown rate, while USD(T) pairs showed a 62.12% breakdown rate. Trend continuation weighed heavily to the bears for both pairs with 74.64% (USD(T)) and 78.87% (BTC) continuation rates for triangles appearing in a downtrend. Symmetrical triangles with a preceding bull trend showed dismal continuation results on BTC pairs with a mere 23.4% continuation rate.

The USD(T) pairs fared better with a majority 52.72% continuation rate. Still, these numbers are notably different from symmetrical triangles in stock markets, which, according to Bulkowski, break upward 60% of the time.[xvi] A clear visual observation from cataloging 400 charts is the presence of symmetrical triangles at the top of bull trends, particularly after several bullish advances.

These findings are exciting and important to crypto traders because applying stock-based statistics may not be as precise. For sure, the sample size in the stock market study was larger but of the available data in the top 100 cryptos, totaling 253 samples, these results undeniably show a clear divergence in findings. As time goes on, I look forward to further tracking the performance of symmetrical triangles.

Price performance for symmetrical triangles showed elevated swings for USD(T) pairs. The USD(T) pairs' unfiltered gains and gains filtering outliers over 400% were considerably higher than those of the BTC paired markets. However, when filtering all gainers above 100%, both pairs were closely matched: USD(T) pairs averaged a 54.06% gain and BTC pairs averaged a 51.15% gain. Average declines were similar at -47.44% (USD(T)) and -44.06% (BTC), which showed only a slightly heavier decline for the USD(T) pairs.

Ascending Triangles

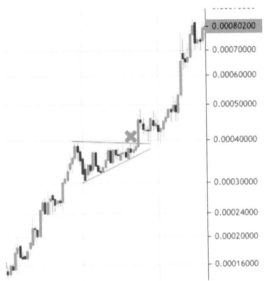

Figure 7.12 Waves/BTC, 1D, March/April 2017, Bittrex (tradingview chart)

Notice the tightly wound consolidation and "retests" before continuation accelerated.

The ascending triangle is marked by its consecutive higher lows and flat top, which roughly creates a right triangle. Generally, I want at least three consecutive lows trending higher forming the support line with the more support touches the better. I give less deference to the resistance line so long as at least two clearly identifiable highs end flat or nearly flat. The support line should touch most of the higher lows, forming a tightening consolidation. The higher lows indicate bullish momentum and the break above the flat top indicates a higher high and departure from the consolidation period.

Table 7.4

Performance Statistics of Ascending Triangles

	USD(T) Traded Pairs	BTC Traded Pairs	Combined Avgs.
# of Examined Patterns	52	26	78
Upside Breakout %	63.46%	50%	56.73%

Downside Breakdown %	36.54%	50%	43.27%
Bullish Trend Continuation % (Preceding Bullish Trend)	66.66%	100%*	83.33%*
Trend Reversal % (Preceding Bullish Trend)	33.34%	0%*	16.67%*
Bearish Trend Continuation % (Preceding Bearish Trend)	43.75%	72.22%	57.98%
Trend Reversal % (Preceding Bearish Trend)	56.25%	27.78%	42.01%
Unfiltered Avg. % Gain from Upside Breakout	247.39%	191.69%	219.54%
Avg. % Decline from Downside Breakdown	-50.94%	-35.76%	-43.35%
Filtered Avg. % Gain from Upside Breakout (Excluding Outliers Over 400%)	133.44%	109.27%	121.35%
Filtered Avg. % Gain from Upside Breakout (Excluding Gainers Over 100%)	64.82%	44.29%	54.55%

Summary of the Findings

Ascending triangles have a reputation for bullish continuation and bullish reversals. Here, the study confirms such bias but with a twist. Both BTC and USD(T) pairs averaged together show the upside breakout rate at 56.73% and trend continuation for ascending triangles with a preceding bullish trend was 83.33%. Overall, this supports the bullish theory, but I emphasize the findings individually are quite different. Ascending triangles in BTC traded pairs with a preceding bearish trend played a significantly greater role in bearish continuations than in the USD(T) counterpart (72.22% vs. 43.75%, respectively). This is precisely the type of detail I am looking for as a trader. Additionally, ascending triangles appeared twice as frequently in USD(T) pairs than BTC pairs.

For USD(T) traded pairs, 63.46% of all examined ascending triangles broke upward, regardless of whether a bullish or bearish trend immediately led up to the pattern. Even better, USD(T) ascending triangles appearing with a preceding bull trend continued that trend 66.66% of the time. Moreover, the USD(T) ascending triangles with a preceding bear trend still staged a bullish reversal 56.25% of the time.

However, when examining the BTC traded pairs, the total breakout vs. breakdown percentages were a coin toss. But, all of the triangles with a preceding bullish trend broke upward! So, how can that be? It's simple: a majority of the ascending triangles found in the Bitcoin traded pairs were preceded by a downtrend. Still, these findings support the theory that ascending triangles found with a preceding bullish trend are more likely to break upward but caution BTC traded ascending triangles preceded by a downtrend appear far more likely to continue down than reverse. Thus, these results again highlight the importance of looking at the data separately depending on whether you are trading against USD(T) or Bitcoin.

In terms of price performance, ascending triangles have big upside potential. Aggregate unfiltered gains totaled an average 219.54% rise for all ascending triangles. USD(T) traded pairs performed better than BTC pairs with average 247.39% vs. 191.69%, respectively. USD(T) traded pairs' superior performance trickled down when filtering the results as well. So, keep that in mind when you see an ascending triangle on a USD(T) pair.

Descending Triangles

Figure 7.13 BTC/USD, 1D, 2018, Coinbase (tradingview chart)
Bitcoin sports two beautiful large and clear descending triangles. The first was a result of an 11-month consolidation following the 2017 bubble peak. The second marked the top of the 2019 recovery.

The descending triangle is the mirror image of an ascending triangle. Rather than a series of higher lows and a flat top, its marked by a series of lower highs and a flat bottom (support line). The descending highs show the buyers' inability to break the bearish trend, and the break below the support line suggests a lower low, departing from the long-standing support level, and thus bearish continuation. Importantly, descending triangles can be both continuations and reversals, and failed descending triangles can break violently the opposite direction. So, while having an overall bearish disposition, the descending triangle can be a big mover in either direction. Still, according to my findings, descending triangles should be viewed with a bearish disposition. As shown in the Figure 7.13 above, both the continuation and reversal favored the bears.

Figure 7.14 BTC/USD, 1D, 2018, Coinbase (tradingview charts)

The descending triangle featured in Figure 7.14 was a result of nearly a year of consolidation following the 2017 Bitcoin bubble peak. It provided one of the best short opportunities in Bitcoin's history because of its protracted and clear development. Note the smaller symmetrical triangle inside the last third of the descending triangle. This provided two clear short opportunities. By shorting both breaks, I averaged my entry and risk while entering a heavier second short below the descending triangle support line. Patterns inside other patterns can offer additional strategic opportunities.

Table 7.5

Performance Statistics of Descending Triangles

	USD(T) Traded Pairs	BTC Traded Pairs	Combined Avgs.
# of Examined Patterns	57	64	121
Upside Breakout %	33.34%	37.5%	35.42%
Downside Breakdown %	66.66%	62.5%	64.58%
Bullish Trend Continuation % (Preceding Bullish Trend)	45.45%	40%	42.72%
Trend Reversal % (Preceding Bullish Trend)	54.55%	60%	57.27%
Bearish Trend Continuation % (Preceding Bearish Trend)	74.28%	65.11%	69.69%
Trend Reversal % (Preceding Bearish Trend)	25.72%	34.89%	30.3%
Unfiltered Avg. % Gain from Upside Breakout	269.07%	103.16%	186.11%
Avg. % Decline from Downside Breakdown	-49.53%	-40.9%	-45.21%
Filtered Avg. % Gain from Upside Breakout (Excluding Outliers Over 400%)	114.80%	71.13%	92.96%
Filtered Avg. % Gain from Upside Breakout (Excluding Gainers Over 100%)	52.66%	54.84%	53.75%

Summary of the Findings

Descending triangles appear to be the bearish heavyweight of the triangle class but when they go against the odds, the upside performance can be impressive. The aggregate breakdown percentage for combined pairs was 64.58%, with little difference when separating the findings (66.66% for USD(T) pairs and 62.5% for BTC pairs). Both USD(T) and BTC traded pairs showed strong bearish follow-through with triangles continuing a preceding bear trend 74.28% and 65.11% of the time, respectively. Notably, neither pair showed a positive breakout correlation with triangles preceded by a bull trend.

Interestingly, USD(T) descending triangles that broke upward against the odds showed striking price action performance. The average unfiltered gain for USD(T) pairs was an impressive 269.07% with a strong majority (68.42%) of breakout descending triangles gaining over 100%. So, please don't assume excluding big gainers necessarily helps with accuracy or realistic expectations! This shows a big upside to descending triangles that fail to break downward in USD(T) pairs.

Unfortunately, the BTC pairs did not perform nearly as well and only saw an average 103.16% breakout gain even including the unfiltered gainers. This same disparity continued when filtering the outliers over 400% with USD(T) pairs averaging 114.80% gains, while the BTC pairs only saw 71.13%. Still, upward breakouts against the odds proved substantial for both categories. On the downside, average declines from breakdowns were -49.53% for USD(T) pairs and -40.9% for BTC pairs. Hence, USD(T) pairs punished bulls more severely.

Wedges

Wedges are often triangular but differ from triangles in that they are pointed upward, downward, or broaden outward. Common wedges include rising wedges, falling wedges, and broadening wedges. Like triangles, I require that wedges have at least five touches collectively on support and resistance lines. Ideally, however, three on each line is preferred. Traditionally, many traders classify falling and rising wedges as reversal patterns. However, despite recognizing and supporting their reversal potential, I put them in this category because they also act as a common continuation pattern.

Falling Wedges

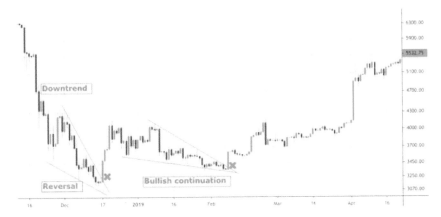

Figure 7.15 BTC/USD, 1D, Nov. 2018 - March 2019, Coinbase (tradingview chart)

The falling wedge is my favorite pattern for a short-term swing trade. I find it highly reliable for a strong bounce but unreliable in the longer-term. Defined by its consecutive lower highs and lower lows that converge into a wedge-shaped point, it appears frequently as a bullish reversal pattern during a downtrend (wedge on the left featured in Figure 7.15) or as a continuation on a bullish retrace (wedge on the right featured in Figure 7.15). As mentioned previously, a wedge shape may be a pennant if it occurs in shorter time frames (less than 21 days). Falling wedges can signal reversal and continuation, but, on either occasion, I target an upside breakout. If compelled to make a target, the top of where the wedge began would be on the high side.

I caution the greatest issue with the falling wedge is a breakout that fails pretty quickly and resumes a downtrend. The performance study below further reinforces and discusses this issue in greater detail. But, for a great example, see the Ethereum chart featured below in Figure 7.16. Despite the failure to sustain the trend, by exercising careful attention or with a trailing stop-loss, this trade still could have netted ~25% (no leverage), and 25% is on the low side of failed breakouts.

Figure 7.16 ETH/USDT, 1D, 2019, Binance (tradingview chart)

Table 7.6

Performance Statistics of Falling Wedges

	USD(T) Traded Pairs	BTC Traded Pairs	Combined Avgs.
# of Examined Patterns	52	49	101
Upside Breakout %	84.61%	81.63%	83.12%
Downside Breakdown %	15.39%	18.37%	16.88%
Bullish Trend Continuation % (Preceding Bullish Trend)	85.71%	87.87%	86.79%
Trend Reversal % (Preceding Bullish Trend)	14.29%	12.13%	13.21%
Bearish Trend Continuation % (Preceding Bearish Trend)	16.66%	29.41%	23.03%
Trend Reversal % (Preceding Bearish Trend)	83.34%	70.59%	79.96%
Unfiltered Avg. % Gain from Upside Breakout	187.97%	150.53%	169.25%
Avg. % Decline from Downside Breakdown	-50.06%	-36.66%	-43.36%

Filtered Avg. % Gain from Upside Breakout (Excluding Outliers Over 400%)	127.81%	102.55%	115.18%
Filtered Avg. % Gain from Upside Breakout (Excluding Gainers Over 100%)	67.45%	46.25%	56.85%

Summary of the Findings

This study confirms what I always thought as a crypto trader, falling wedges are overwhelmingly bullish on all accounts. The upside potential is clear as 83.12% of all falling wedges broke upward (81.61% of USD(T) pairs and 81.63% of BTC pairs). Not surprisingly, 85.71% of USD(T) and 87.87% of BTC falling wedges with preceding bull trends continued the trend. Finally, the reversal potential is obvious as 83.34% of falling wedges in USD(T) traded pairs reversed a bearish trend. Similarly, in BTC traded pairs, only 29.41% of falling wedges continued a bearish trend, while 70.59% staged a reversal.

However, as I alluded to above, these bullish breakouts and reversals may be short-lived. For BTC traded pairs, two-thirds of reversals breaking upward from a preceding downtrend failed quickly, and both BTC and USD(T) pairs had scores of wedges that failed to make it halfway back to the wedge top or sustain an enduring breakout beyond a quick pop. Still, despite failing to result in dependable sustained breakouts, these wedges provided a consistent breakout pop.

In terms of overall price action compared with other patterns in the study, the unfiltered and filtered gains were moderate. So, keep this in mind when trading falling wedges. Still, SIA led the outlier pack with a beautiful 1,760% USD(T) gainer.

In sum, the study supports my theory that falling wedges are an excellent short-term breakout trade, but they should be met with caution and profit-taking stop-losses should be set quickly after the initial breakout.

It's clear, falling wedges are good for a short-term pop but cannot be relied on consistently for anything further.

Rising Wedges

Figure 7.17 BTC/USD, 1D, 2020, Coinbase (tradingview chart)
Two opportunities to short BTC/USD here: the first at trend break or again at the retest of the broken support line.

The rising wedge is the bearish version of the falling wedge, and also makes for a fantastic swing trade opportunity. Rising wedges that occur in an uptrend may intuitively look bullish with consecutive higher highs and higher lows that converge into a wedge-shaped point. Despite the bullish appearance, the rising wedge is a classic bearish reversal and continuation pattern. Only on rare occasions do they break upward. Often, rising wedges appear as a top during an uptrend signaling reversal or as the top of a bounce during a downtrend signaling bearish continuation. Breakout is confirmed below the support line. For target loving traders, I first look to the lowest low creating the wedge.

Table 7.7

Performance Statistics of Rising Wedges

	USD(T) Traded Pairs	BTC Traded Pairs	Combined Avgs.
# of Examined Patterns	36	28	64
Upside Breakout %	8.33%	14.28%	11.3%

Downside Breakdown %	91.67%	85.72%	88.69%
Bullish Trend Continuation % (Preceding Bullish Trend)	15%	7.15%	11.07%
Trend Reversal % (Preceding Bullish Trend)	85%	92.85%	88.92%
Bearish Trend Continuation % (Preceding Bearish Trend)	100%*	78.57%	89.28%*
Trend Reversal % (Preceding Bearish Trend)	0%*	21.43%	10.71%*
Unfiltered Avg. % Gain from Upside Breakout	138.83%	67.87%	103.35%
Avg. % Decline from Downside Breakdown	-51.68%	-49.77%	-50.72%
Filtered Avg. % Gain from Upside Breakout (Excluding Outliers Over 400%)	138.83%	67.87%	103.35%
Filtered Avg. % Gain from Upside Breakout (Excluding Gainers Over 100%)	86.25%	48.16%	67.2%

Summary of the Findings

Opposite to the falling wedge, the rising wedge is dominantly bearish. A whopping 91.67% of all USD(T) rising wedges broke downward, while 85.72% of the BTC pairs broke downward. Both pairs showed strong bearish continuation tendencies with 100% of all USD(T) and 78.57% of all BTC pairs continuing a preceding bearish trend. Notably, this 100% statistic is likely due to the limited sample size but it's safe to say rising wedges strongly favor bearish continuation here. Both pairs also showed strong bearish reversal potential with patterns preceded by bullish trends breaking downward 85% (USD(T)) and 92.85% (BTC) of the time. Regarding the price action performance, the unfiltered and filtered price gains are relatively low compared to other patterns, meaning don't expect a major push even if a rising wedge breaks upward. BTC pairs performed notably worse than USD(T) pairs.

Broadening Wedges

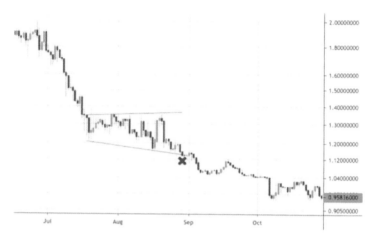

Figure 7.18 LEO/USD, 1D, 2019, Bitfinex (tradingview chart)

The broadening wedge is the opposite of a regular wedge. Rather than support and resistance lines converging, trend lines repel, creating a widening fan shape. If sporting a fan that points upward, regardless of the immediately preceding trend trajectory (up or down), with higher highs and flat or higher lows, it's called an ascending broadening wedge. If the fan is facing downward with lower lows and flat or lower highs, it's a descending broadening wedge (exemplified above in Figure 7.18). Notably, I do not distinguish broadening wedges further based on angles like some traders do.

Generally, if the support and resistance line are both trending the same direction, it signals a continuation pattern bias. However, if the wedge support line and resistance line are symmetrical going opposite directions (one up one down), then it may be construed as a broadening top or bottom, which can be a reversal signal and is detailed in the tops and bottoms section.

Similar to other patterns like triangles, I seek a minimum five touches on the support and resistance lines. A break above the resistance line or below the support line marks the entry. Be careful setting stop-losses on broadening wedges, as the opposing trend line is likely too far from the initial breakout/breakdown for a reasonable stop-loss. I often set a stop-loss inside the wedge but comfortably beyond the freshly broken trend line.

Figure 7.19 BTC/USD, 1D, 2019, Coinbase (tradingview charts)
Here is a clear example of a forming and completed broadening wedge from Bitcoin in Spring 2019. Notice how both trend lines are supported by higher highs and lows, which means it's an ascending broadening wedge. Also, note the breakout volume.

Table 7.8

Performance Statistics of Broadening Wedges

	USD(T) Traded Pairs	BTC Traded Pairs	Combined Avgs.
# of Examined Patterns	23	17	40
Upside Breakout %	47.83%	47.05%	47.44%
Downside Breakdown %	52.17%	52.95%	52.56%
Ascending Wedge Bullish Trend Continuation %	80%	100%*	90%*

(Preceding Bullish Trend)			
Ascending Wedge Bearish Trend Continuation % (Preceding Bearish Trend)	100%*	85.71%	92.85%*
Descending Wedge Bullish Trend Continuation % (Preceding Bullish Trend)	50%	100%*	75%*
Descending Wedge Bearish Trend Continuation % (Preceding Bearish Trend)	66.66%	50%	58.33%
Unfiltered Avg. % Gain from Upside Breakout	213.4%	87.87%	150.63%
Avg. % Decline from Downside Breakdown	-42.12%	-48.16%	-45.14%
Filtered Avg. % Gain from Upside Breakout (Excluding Outliers Over 400%)	149.75%	87.87%	118.81%
Filtered Avg. % Gain from Upside Breakout (Excluding Gainers Over 100%)	56.7%	36%	46.35%

Summary of the Findings

The available data is pretty low to draw anything conclusive. However, the total breakout vs. breakdown averages show that broadening wedges on the whole are a pretty neutral pattern. While the results indicate a high degree of continuation for ascending broadening wedges, the data is too small to apply those numbers strictly. I would simply say the results show a notion of bias toward continuation for ascending broadening wedges.

Price action for descending broadening wedges in USD(T) pairs was exceptional, despite the small sample size. Of the 12 examined descending broadening wedges, all wedges preceded by a bull trend that broke out positively rose more than 200% with an average gain of 373.4%.

Top and Bottom Reversals

Reversal patterns indicate the current prevailing trend and market forces (buyers or sellers) are running out of steam and a trend change is imminent. Sometimes a reversal indicates a temporary trend change, while for others it may indicate a long-term bottom or top. In many cases, it may be hard to tell the difference. Nevertheless, even a shorter-term reversal play can be very lucrative.

Double Tops

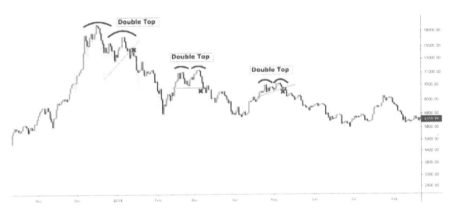

Figure 7.20 BTC/USD, 1D, 2017, Coinbase (tradingview chart)
This Bitcoin example exhibits three double tops related to the deflating of the 2017 bubble. The first slightly uneven top marked the end of the run, while the second and third evenly matched double tops marked the reversal of the first and second major bounces.

A double top occurs when buyers make a new high, lose control but recover a sell-off quickly, and then print an equal or slightly unequal second high. The double top indicates buyer exhaustion and inability to carry the positive trend further. Some traders are strict about the highs being precisely equal or near to it, but I have found slightly unbalanced highs just as reliable. Essentially, they show the same thing: buyers' inability to push the asset price beyond the last high. Double tops are common in crypto and can mark the top of a sustained uptrend or significant bounce.

Sell or short signals are formed by a break below a diagonal or flat neckline. When possible, I like to draw my neckline from a diagonal trend of higher lows formed with the second top if wicks are present rather than at the valley low. Notably, many traders often use only the valley low as the neckline, which is flat rather than slanted. My strategy tends to be on the more aggressive side. However, in some instances if no diagonal neckline is present, I use the valley low. Additionally, another way I sometimes play a double top, if it occurs within a short time frame (not many weeks/months apart), is to short or sell at the second high after the first red-bodied candle closes below a reversal candle. For example, after a bearish confirmation candle following a spinning top, gravestone doji, shooting star, or another reversal-leaning candle. Then, I put a stop-loss above the recent high. This strategy is riskier in that the pattern is technically not confirmed; however, the entry is often much better.

Figure 7.21
(tradingview chart)

Link/USDT, 1D, 2020, Binance

The left example comes from the Link/USDT pair and shows a sharp and quick selloff following two near equal highs. Notice the riskier unconfirmed sell opportunity after a shooting star, hanging man, and full-bodied red candle.

In this instance, waiting for confirmation on the second opportunity would have resulted in missing the move. Still, there will always be another!

Table 7.9

Performance Statistics of Double Tops

	USD(T) Traded Pairs	BTC Traded Pairs	Combined Avgs.
# of Examined Patterns	26	20	46
Avg. % Decline	-71.88%	-63.05%	-67.46%

Summary of the Findings (omitted)

Double Bottoms

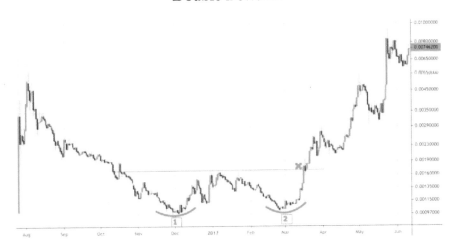

Figure 7.22 ETC/BTC, 1D, 2016/17, Bittrex (tradingview chart)

Inverse to the double top, a double bottom occurs when sellers make a new low, lose control but sink a following rally quickly, and then print an equal or slightly unequal second low. The double bottom indicates seller exhaustion and inability to carry the trend further to a new low. As with the double top, I play slightly uneven double bottoms the same. Double bottoms frequently mark the bottom of a sustained downtrend or significant dip. Long or buy signals are formed by a break above either a diagonal or flat neckline.

Table 7.10

Performance Statistics of Double Bottoms

	USD(T) Traded Pairs	BTC Traded Pairs	Combined Avgs.
# of Examined Patterns	23	25	48
Unfiltered Avg. % Gain from Upside Breakout	258.15%	230.66%	244.4%
Filtered Avg. % Gain from Upside Breakout (Excluding Outliers Over 400%)	126.25%	138.1%	132.17%
Filtered Avg. % Gain from Upside Breakout (Excluding Gainers Over 100%)	87.25%	72.37%	79.81%

Summary of the Findings

While the sample size isn't huge, I find it very impressive the combined average of 48 double bottoms was 244.4% in unfiltered gains. To put that into perspective, only 25% of USD(T) and 36.6% of BTC pairs sampled were under the 100% gain threshold. Undeniably, double bottoms are a triple-digit winner in this study of the crypto markets. I also found it interesting that averages filtering outliers over 400% favored BTC pair performance – escaping the persistent superior performance of USD(T) pairs seen in this study.

The "Adam" and "Eve" Classification

Some traders distinguish the type of double top or bottom based on the shape of each low.[xvii] If the low displays a V shape it's an "Adam," while a U shape is an "Eve." For example, the "Adam and Eve" double bottom is recognizable by two differently shaped lows with the first being steeper and pointier than the rounder second (see Figure 7.23). Double tops and bottoms with this classification can thus be "Adam and Eve," "Adam and Adam," "Eve and Adam," or "Eve and Eve."

Figure 7.23 KNC/USD c., 1D, 2018/19, Binance (tradingview chart)
This chart displays an "Adam and Eve" double bottom.

Head and Shoulders Tops

Figure 7.24 XEM/USD c., 1D, 2017/18, Bittrex (tradingview chart)

The head and shoulders (HS) reversal pattern is a classic trader favorite. Distinguished by the shape of a head and its shoulders formed by three highs with the middle being the highest and both surrounding highs being lower, but at equal or near equal levels. The HS reversal is found in an uptrend and shows the buyers' inability to make three consecutive higher highs and sellers securing a critical lower high. The lows below the head and shoulders are connected to create a support line, which creates the "neckline." The breakdown below the neckline should be targeted for entry.

Table 7.11

Performance Statistics of Head and Shoulders Tops

	USD(T) Traded Pairs	BTC Traded Pairs	Combined Avgs.
# of Examined Patterns	11	10	21
Avg. % Decline	-70.59%	-69.9%	-70.24%

Summary of the Findings

Again, a small sample size that shouldn't be taken as gospel, but I find it interesting that the breakdown percentage was within 1% for both pairs. As much as I wish for an abundance of samples, the chart history is limited and we will have to wait for further charts to be examined and greater price history.

Inverted Head and Shoulders Bottoms

Figure 7.25 BTC/USD, 1D, 2019, Coinbase (tradingview chart)

The inverted head and shoulders (IHS) is the bullish counterpart to the head and shoulders reversal. Following a sustained downtrend, three lows are printed with the middle one being lowest and accompanied by two similarly higher lows, which creates the appearance of an inverted head and two shoulders. The IHS shows the sellers' inability to continue the trend with three consecutive lower lows and the buyers securing a critical higher low. Connecting the peaks/highs of the failed rallies between the lows creates the neckline. The breakout above the neckline

111

should be targeted for entry.

Table 7.12

Performance Statistics of Inverted Head and Shoulders Bottoms

	USD(T) Traded Pairs	BTC Traded Pairs	Combined Avgs.
# of Examined Patterns	3	5	8
Unfiltered Avg. % Gain from Upside Breakout	114%	89.1%	101.55%
Filtered Avg. % Gain from Upside Breakout (Excluding Outliers Over 400%)	114%	89.1%	101.55%
Filtered Avg. % Gain from Upside Breakout (Excluding Gainers Over 100%)	88.5%	66.83%	77.66%

Summary of the Findings (omitted)

Rounding Tops

Figure 7.26 REP/BTC, 1D, 2017, Poloniex (tradingview chart)

The rounding top is marked by a series of highs that trend upward before turning downward creating an inverted bowl-like shape. The rounding top shows buyers failing to make consecutive new highs and momentum visibly diminishes in a rounding fashion. Similar to other top patterns, a diagonal or lateral neckline is used to mark the sell point or short entry. As mentioned, I prefer diagonal necklines when possible because the entry is usually better but with a slightly higher appetite for risk.

Table 7.13

Performance Statistics of Rounding Tops

	USD(T) Traded Pairs	BTC Traded Pairs	Combined Avgs.
# of Examined Patterns	7	3	10
Avg. % Decline	-62.35%	-72.5%	-67.42%

Summary of the Findings (omitted)

Rounding Bottoms

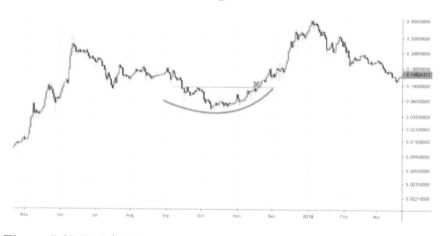

Figure 7.27 BTS/USD c., 1D, 2017, Poloniex (tradingview chart)

The rounding bottom is marked by a series of lows that trend downward before turning upward creating a bowl-like shape. The rounding bottom shows sellers failing to drive the price to consecutive new lows and sell power visibly diminishes in a rounding fashion. Same as the rounding top and other patterns, a diagonal or lateral neckline is used to mark the entry.

Table 7.14

Performance Statistics of Rounding Bottoms

	USD(T) Traded Pairs	BTC Traded Pairs	Combined Avgs.
# of Examined Patterns	7	14	21
Unfiltered Avg. % Gain from Upside Breakout	630%	408.46%	519.23%
Filtered Avg. % Gain from Upside Breakout (Excluding Outliers Over 400%)	185.2%	157.27%	171.24%
Filtered Avg. % Gain from Upside Breakout (Excluding Gainers Over 100%)	N/A	48.66%	N/A

Summary of the Findings

Despite the small sample size, which of course should not be ignored, the unfiltered gains of both pairs are striking. However, removing several outliers, some with quadruple digits, brings the performance back down to earth – at least relative to crypto. Notably however, all USD(T) pairs and nearly all of the BTC pairs marked gains over 100%.

Triple Tops

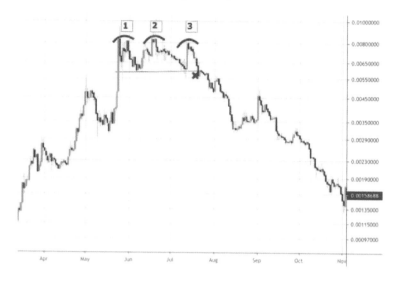

Figure 7.28 ETC/BTC, 1D, 2017, Bittrex (tradingview chart)

The triple top is similar to a double top but with three equal or near equal highs and two valleys in between. Triple tops are also similar to a head and shoulders top with the difference being a head and shoulders has two lower highs and one higher high in the middle. Triple tops in all markets are an infrequent occurrence. I only identified a handful of them in the BTC pairs and none at all in the USD(T) pairs. Still, traders should be aware of its existence.

Table 7.15

Performance Statistics of Triple Tops

	USD(T) Traded Pairs	BTC Traded Pairs	Combined Avgs.
# of Examined Patterns	N/A	5	N/A
Avg. % Decline	N/A	-80.2%	N/A

Summary of the Findings (omitted)

Triple Bottoms

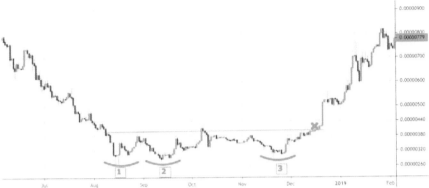

Figure 7.29 TRX/BTC, 1D, 2018, Binance (tradingview chart)

The triple bottom is the counterpart to the triple top. As such, the triple bottom is similar to the double bottom but with three equal or near equal lows and two failed rallies in between. Triple bottoms are also similar to inverted head and shoulders but with equal lows rather than two equal and one lowest. Triple bottoms are also rare and only appeared in the BTC pairs.

Table 7.16

Performance Statistics of Triple Bottoms

	USD(T) Traded Pairs	BTC Traded Pairs	Combined Avgs.
# of Examined Patterns	N/A	4	N/A
Unfiltered Avg. % Gain from Upside Breakout	N/A	72.37%	N/A
Filtered Avg. % Gain from Upside Breakout (Excluding Outliers Over 400%)	N/A	72.37%	N/A
Filtered Avg. % Gain from Upside Breakout (Excluding Gainers Over 100%)	N/A	35.25%	N/A

Broadening Tops and Bottoms
(Symmetrical Broadening Wedges)

Figure 7.30 DCR/BTC, 1D, 2017/18, Bittrex (tradingview chart)
Notice the two opportunities to long this broadening bottom: first at the trend break of the retracement (lower x) and again at the breakout of the level that last touched the resistance line (higher x).

Broadening tops and bottoms are a symmetrical broadening wedge that frequently signals reversal. Traders may also call them inverted or inverse symmetrical triangles or megaphone tops and bottoms. Rather than support or resistance lines creating a fan that points upward or downward, broadening tops and bottoms are formed when the wedge fans outward symmetrically. Often, they come with a retrace (from the top) or failed rally (from the bottom) into the wedge before the ultimate breakout or breakdown. Traders can enter at the breakout/breakdown of the support/resistance, or, if a retracement exists, when the price breaches the level where the trend line was last touched. Additionally, like in Figure 7.30 above, if the retracement has a clear trend line, then a long from the trend line break with a stop-loss below the retrace low is possible (or vice versa for a short). In my study, I noted several occasions where broadening tops or bottoms failed and played out like a continuation pattern.

Table 7.17

Performance Statistics of Broadening Tops

	USD(T) Traded Pairs	BTC Traded Pairs	Combined Avgs.
# of Examined Patterns	N/A	2	N/A
Avg. % Decline	N/A	-43%	N/A

Summary of the Findings (omitted)

Table 7.18

Performance Statistics of Broadening Bottoms

	USD(T) Traded Pairs	BTC Traded Pairs	Combined Avgs.
# of Examined Patterns	N/A	3	N/A
Unfiltered Avg. % Gain from Upside Breakout	N/A	169.83%	N/A
Filtered Avg. % Gain from Upside Breakout (Excluding Outliers Over 400%)	N/A	91.25%	N/A
Filtered Avg. % Gain from Upside Breakout (Excluding Gainers Over 100%)	N/A	91.25%	N/A

Summary of the Findings (omitted)

Evolving Charts (Failed Patterns, Changing Shapes, & Reading a Chart Fluidly)

The importance of waiting for clear and evolved patterns cannot be overstated. Rushing into a trade because you are over eager is one of the easiest ways to lose money. If you need to strongly justify why a chart pattern is what you say it is, it may mean it's not a very clear pattern.

Similarly, calling and entering a pattern before it's formed because that's what you want to happen is equally troublesome.

However, even if a pattern does not meet its most rigid definition but looks pretty darn close, it may still behave in a similar manner. Keep in mind when examining, say, a triangular consolidation, you are just observing a tightening range of price action. The breakout simply shows a departure from the spring-wound lull period. So, in some instances whether the pattern is perfectly defined may not matter. Still, as a general rule, I do not take a trade unless the pattern is screaming at me how obvious its behavioral disposition is and that I'd be a fool not to take it.

Additionally, do not let your bias on how you think something is going to play out blind you from when the price action is not conforming to your theory. In other words, read a chart in a dynamic manner where you are willing to be wrong, to change your opinion, and to act on changing opinions. Even if a pattern dominantly plays out in one direction, the minority actor still exists.

Patterns frequently complete and quickly evolve into different forms. It's your job as a trader to keep up with the evolution of price action. A bearish pennant may break down but then consolidate into a bullish triangle as time goes by. A continuation one day may begin to form a reversal the next. Finally, the patterns described in this book are only a select few and do not encompass all existing and commonly recognized patterns. These are just some core patterns every trader should know. So, I urge traders to further research and incorporate patterns as they see fit!

Chart Pattern Takeaways:

1. Chart patterns are repeatedly observable patterns found in all markets, which allow traders to predict future movements of price action with reasonable success.

2. Continuation patterns suggest a trend continuation bias but can break either way.

3. Performance statistics help traders understand pattern behavior, but no pattern is guaranteed to behave the same way.

4. Areas where pattern performance differs between BTC and USD(T) pairs may offer traders particularly valuable insights.

5. Patterns are dynamic and evolving and should be read as such.

CHAPTER 8:

OSCILLATORS AND

MOMENTUM GAUGES

An oscillator is a technical tool that travels concurrently with the general price action of an asset showing some corresponding data or data relationship. Oscillators are displayed as a line that travels (oscillates) between two values. Often, oscillators try to show momentum, market health or condition, buy or sell points, or other information useful to a trader. Over the years, traders have created dozens of oscillators measuring all sorts of data and data trends. Some of the most popular oscillators include, RSI, MACD, and Stochastic RSI. For this trading strategy, I only focus on the RSI.

Relative Strength Index (RSI)

Figure 8.1 The RSI traveling below the price action section of a chart. (tradingview excerpt)

For my trading strategy, no oscillator is more useful than the Relative Strength Index or "RSI," which was developed and published by J. Welles Wilder in his 1978 book, *New Concepts in Technical Trading Systems.*[xviii] In sum, the RSI is a momentum indicator that measures strength of buying and selling by calculating average gains and losses relative to each other over an examined period of time (usually 14 periods). The RSI is displayed as a line that travels between 0 and 100 and is usually placed below the price action portion of the chart. The RSI gives useful readings on price action and offers an outlook on whether conditions are bearish, bullish, oversold, or overbought. The most useful aspect of the RSI for many traders is identifying divergences between the highs and lows of the oscillator and those of an asset's price. An identified divergence often predicts trend changes or continuations. This section briefly focuses on the basics of reading the RSI and dedicates several subsections to divergences.

When the RSI is under 50, it's in bear territory. Conversely, an RSI over 50 marks bull territory. When the RSI is above 70, the asset is considered overbought at that time, while an RSI under 30 is oversold. Importantly, overbought and oversold conditions can remain for long periods of time while an asset's price continues with the trend during strong bull or bear cycles. Some traders use the RSI as a buy or sell indicator based on when it reaches the overbought or oversold levels. The difficulty with gauging the RSI bottom or top is you don't know it until after it passes, and the RSI may range in oversold or overbought territory for a while. Thus, many traders prefer to make an RSI-based entry when it travels back into normal range from the overbought or oversold level (into the purple range from the white). Still, that entry may be poorly timed if a price divergence is forming. I tend to keep these levels in mind and the overall RSI disposition is often helpful when combined with other aspects of technical analysis, but I rarely enter a position simply because the RSI is overextended.

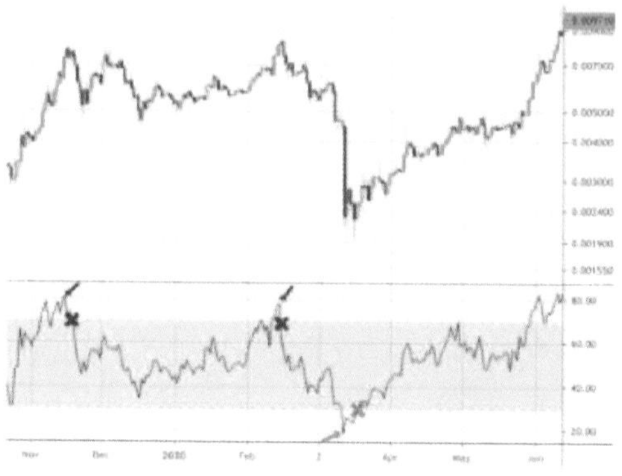

Figure 8.2
(tradingview chart)

VET/USDT, 1D, 2019/20, Binance

In this example, you can see the RSI traveling below the price action over approximately eight months. Notice how the overbought high of 81 and second high around 77 both correspond with local tops. Similarly, the recent bottom stops in oversold territory right below 20.

Also note the three potential entries for trades based on over-extended conditions. On the first one (the red x on the left), the price rebounded quickly. It would not have been a great entry like the second or third.

Divergences

By far, the most important indicator for my trading strategy is recognizing and understanding divergences that occur between a crypto's price and a momentum oscillator. Identifying a divergence can assist with predicting trend changes and continuations. I like to think of divergences as supporting evidence, which almost always coincide with other aspects of technical analysis. In other words, they are particularly useful when used in conjunction with other techniques like candlesticks, chart patterns, and trend lines or channels.

A divergence occurs when an asset's highs or lows conflict or diverge from the corresponding highs or lows on the oscillator. There are four types of divergences. Two are bullish: bullish divergence and hidden bullish divergence. Two are bearish: bearish divergence and hidden bearish divergence. Importantly, divergences can also be identified and interpreted similarly with other oscillators like the Stoch RSI or MACD but those are not a focus of this handbook.

Divergences are so important and so frequently used in this trading strategy, it's important to commit them to memory as soon as possible. Divergences are useful on all time frames whether you are trading a scalp on five-minute candles or a large trend shift on daily candles. However, as with all methods in this strategy, I prefer using them on larger time frames like 1D and 4H. This section teaches the types of divergences and how to recognize them before giving examples of where divergences played out as expected. Finally, this section describes several instances where traders should be cautious using divergences and highlights examples of divergences that did not pan out as expected.

Bullish Divergences

The bullish divergence is a trader's best friend. It's a welcome sign when markets go south and often indicates a positive reversal. A bullish divergence occurs in a downtrend when the **price of an asset prints a lower low(s), but the oscillator displays higher low(s).** It's easy to recognize on any chart and it's a proven favorite for me when trading Bitcoin or other cryptos. Bullish divergences are most valuable in my opinion when they occur after a protracted downtrend and appear on large frame charts (4H, 1D, or even 1W).

Figure 8.3
(tradingview chart)

ETH/USD, 1D, 2018, Coinbase

This ETH/USD example shows, during a steep plunge, the price going down with lower lows while the RSI trended up with higher lows. This is a classic bullish divergence. Note the inverted hammer right before reversal.

Here, the low was $80, while the high of the bounce was ~$155. Playing this divergence could have resulted in a 90%+ gain without leverage.

Hidden Bullish Divergences

The hidden bullish divergence is a useful indicator for determining whether to keep playing a chart that is already engaged in a bullish move. In other words, it's an indicator of the underlying strength of a bullish trend. A hidden bullish divergence occurs when an asset's **price makes**

a higher low(s), but the oscillator makes a lower low(s). Generally speaking, a hidden bullish divergence signals that buyers continue to dominate sellers and a continuation in the immediate future is likely.

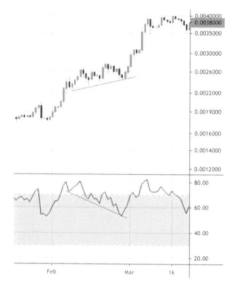

Figure 8.4
(tradingview chart)

BNB/BTC, 1D, 2019, Binance

This example highlights a hidden bullish divergence on a daily time frame. The strong bullish trend printed higher lows while the RSI printed lower lows. This divergence correctly suggested another imminent upward thrust.

Bearish Divergences

A bearish divergence is the bane of the bull, but it's equally as useful as a bullish divergence. This divergence is the counterpart to the bullish divergence and shows a bullish trend losing momentum. A bearish divergence is easily identified when **the price of an asset makes a higher high(s), but the oscillator makes a lower high(s).** Bearish divergences can signal a strong sell signal and often appear at the end of bull trends marking a complete reversal. A bearish divergence may also precede a significant dip during a bull trend or a local top on a bear trend bounce and provide a short-term trade opportunity.

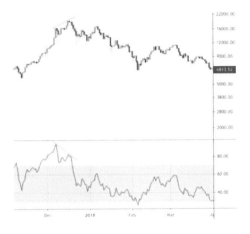

Figure 8.5
(tradingview chart)

BTC/USD, 1D, 2017/18, Kraken

This bearish divergence signaled the epic collapse of the 2017 Bitcoin bull run. On the 1D chart, you can see that last charge of the bulls to nearly $20,000 before crashing down to just under $6,000 in less than two months.

Hidden Bearish Divergences

As you may guess, the hidden bearish divergence is indicative of the strength of an underlying bearish trend. Hidden bearish divergences show the strength of sellers out pacing buyers and the immediate future of the trend is likely to continue down. A hidden bearish divergence is identified when the **price makes a lower high(s), but the oscillator makes a higher high(s).**

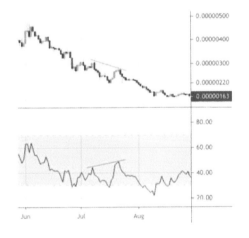

Figure 8.6
(tradingview chart)

TRX/BTC, 1D, 2019, Binance

Here you can see Tron caught in a downtrend against Bitcoin. Note the lower high where the bulls failed to break the trend accompanied by the higher high on the RSI. This example shows a textbook hidden bearish divergence continuation.

126

Weighing Strength of Divergences

Strength of divergences should be considered. As a general rule, the more noticeable the divergence, the greater its significance. Noticeability refers to the steepness of a line's slope, divergence length, and whether it exists on multiple time frames. A flatter line on the oscillator shows less strength than a steep incline or decline. Divergences that last for long periods of time with multiple peaks are more significant than tiny blips that are hard to identify on a chart. Finally, a divergence appearing on multiple time frames (i.e. 4H, 1D, and 1W) is stronger than one that exists in a single time frame.

With these considerations in mind, a slight divergence is still a divergence. Moreover, in some cases you might have a flattening RSI on an asset that is gaining value. Even though it might not be a bearish divergence officially because the RSI is not going down, it's important to understand a flattening RSI may indeed show buyers are weakening. The inverse of that is also true. Finally, not every reversal or continuation will be marked by a divergence! Divergences merely show discrepancies between price trend and relative power of buyers or sellers over an examined period of time; at any period, a big buyer or seller could appear and change the equation. Thus, it's critical for a trader to understand what the momentum gauge means beyond the most obvious signals. In many instances, chart reading is nuanced and with no crystal-clear signal, and many good trades still exist and suggest reversal or continuation even if the RSI does not.

Divergences in Action

Example 1: Bitcoin Bullish Divergences (2019-2020)

BEFORE

Figure 8.7 XBT/USD, 1D and 1W, 2019, Bitmex (tradingview charts)
Notice the protracted bullish divergence on the 1D chart on top. Also, look carefully at the 1W bullish divergence that formed when Bitcoin last touched the support line and confirmed with a bullish hammer.

Figure 8.8 XBT/USD, 1D, 2019/20, Bitmex (tradingview chart)

I highlight this trade in Figures 8.7 and 8.8 because a bullish divergence is apparent on both the daily and weekly time frames. Weekly time frame divergences are a rare occurrence for crypto's brief history, and I tend to give them a lot of deference. This provided two divergence-based long opportunities ("1" and "2" on Figure 8.8). The first 1D bullish divergence played out but failed after a significant rise and trend channel fakeout, creating a longer protracted divergence.

Regarding the second opportunity highlighted in Figure 8.8, a more conservative trader may have waited for the trend channel to break, while a more aggressive trader may have longed near the trend channel support line or at the neckline break of the inverted head and shoulders reversal pattern within the trend channel. Finally, notice how the breakout created a new narrower trend channel with a flattening and slightly overbought RSI. The breakdown from the smaller trend channel was the logical place to take profit because it was supported by multiple technical indicators (a trend channel support line break and flattening/overbought RSI) suggesting a shift in the trend.

Example 2: Ethereum Hidden Bullish Divergence (early 2019)

BEFORE

Figure 8.9 ETH/USDT, 1D, 2019, Binance (tradingview chart)
The triangle was highlighted here rather than the price divergence. However, a clear hidden bullish divergence is visible on the RSI and low just before the triangle.

AFTER

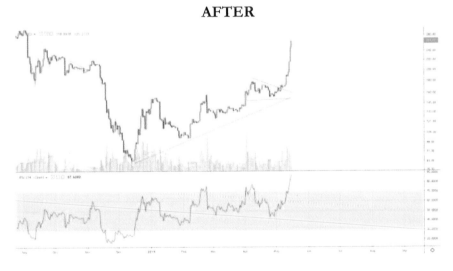

Figure 8.10 ETH/USDT, 1D, 2019, Binance (tradingview chart)

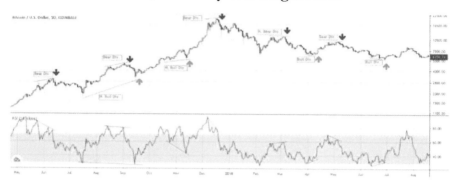

Figure 8.11 BTC/USD, 1D, 2017/18, Coinbase (tradingview chart) Look at how many successful trades could be made simply by entering a position based on 1D RSI divergences. Divergences marked nearly every major trend change during this period. Also note, on the daily frame, Bitcoin rarely traveled into oversold territory during these years and was frequently overbought.

When to Be Careful With Divergences

While divergences are an extremely useful tool, like anything in trading, they do not guarantee a move in the market and only suggest one. Remember, a divergence only shows a momentary discrepancy between the trend (up or down) and the relative power of the buyers or sellers over the examined period of time. Divergences can be invalidated and also change. Often, the divergence itself is not the buy or sell signal but it's used as supporting evidence in conjunction with another buy or sell signal like a trend or pattern breakout. This section identifies a few of the shortcomings new traders should be aware of when using divergences.

Protracted Divergences

First, divergences can last a long time and price action can slump or pump significantly while one is present. In Figure 8.12 below, overeager traders would have been punished severely for longing at the first sight of a bull divergence. Still, a trader who triggered a buy too early but had a tight stop-loss could have mitigated losses or even sold on the bounce. While ultimately this divergence did play out, in instances like this, combining other methods of TA and risk management is critical.

Consider how a trend channel or resistance line on top of the bottom consolidation period may have assisted with this trade. Protracted divergences can be great opportunities, so long as you come across them late in formation or you wisely wait for supporting signals.

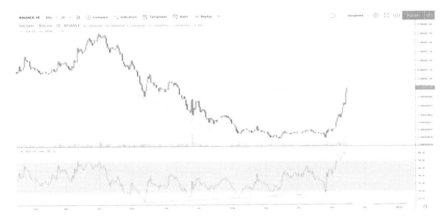

Figure 8.12 VET/BTC, 1D, 2019, Binance (tradingview chart)

Conflicting or Competing Divergences

Second, it's important to note how divergences often bleed into each other. Or in some cases, there may be concurrent or competing divergences. For instance, bearish divergences often turn into hidden bullish divergences and vice versa. When confronted with conflicting divergences, it's a challenge to guess how they will resolve. In Figure 8.13 below, competing divergences resolved with no clear winner or significant and immediate trade opportunity. The resolution resulted in a consolidation within a narrow price range.

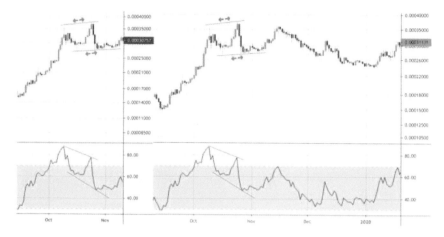

Figure 8.13 Link/BTC, 1D, 2019, Binance (tradingview charts)
Link exhibiting conflicting bearish and hidden bullish divergences resulting in a stalemate and no significant trade opportunity.

Competing Divergence Risk Analysis

When examining competing divergences, I weigh three things: 1) the order in which they appear, favoring the most recent divergence as the one in play; 2) the size of the divergence, giving the larger one or the one most apparent on multiple time frames more weight (see the previous section on weighing divergences); and 3) the general context of the chart structure and other elements of TA. The analysis will depend on the totality of the circumstances for each trade. Keep in mind, conflicting divergences show that buyers and sellers are battling for control of the market. A competing or conflicting divergence, if it's a decisive factor, may be a cautionary note singing uncertainty about price behavior in the near future. Consequently, it may invalidate the reason why you want the trade in the first place: *to act on a strong inclination that the market will behave a certain way imminently.*

Unsolidified Divergences

Third, it's important to let a divergence set. Often times I find myself looking at a chart with a potential divergence forming but not solidified. All too often, these divergences never end up manifesting and entering early may result in a loss. At a minimum, I consider a divergence to be set when the low or high on the oscillator has a bent "v" or "^" shape coinciding with at least one completed candlestick. I often wait for another consecutive candle or two to support the trend movement the divergence suggests. Complimentary candlestick formations are useful to help affirm a divergence. For instance, a bullish hammer where the RSI paints a low point.

Divergence Takeaways:

1. RSI measures momentum and shows overbought and oversold conditions (above 70 and below 30, respectively).

2. RSI divergences help predict trend reversals and continuations and should be construed as supporting evidence in conjunction with other aspects of technical analysis.

3. Divergences are particularly useful on larger time frames.

4. The more noticeable the divergence, the greater its significance.

5. Traders should be mindful of protracted, conflicting, and unsolidified divergences.

CHAPTER 9:
MOVING AVERAGES

Figure 9.1 Moving averages crossing each other. (tradingview excerpt)

A moving average is a technical indicator displayed as a colored line(s) that averages price action over a select period of time. Conceptually, the averaging of an asset's price action helps level out volatility and establishes a clearer trend. Like the RSI, moving averages follow along the price of an asset concurrently. However, unlike the RSI, moving averages are layered directly on the primary chart. Traders often use moving averages to determine levels of support or resistance. For instance, a trader may predict an asset will find support at a moving average traveling below the current price or resistance at a moving average traveling above it. You can set a moving average to measure any period length under any time frame, but for this section I am speaking in periods measured on the 1D chart. Traders frequently use the fifty-day and two-hundred-day moving averages (MA 50 and 200 setting on the 1D chart). My trade strategy does not often use moving averages. However, if a moving average signal like a "death cross" or "golden cross" occurs, which I explain below, I may examine it as supporting evidence of a major trend shift. Despite not using moving averages regularly, I describe them briefly here because they are a popular and useful tool that traders should be aware of.

The Death Cross and Golden Cross

Moving average crosses are a popular signal for major trend changes. A "death cross" occurs when an asset's short-term moving average crosses below its long-term moving average. The death cross most commonly refers to the fifty-day moving average crossing below the two-hundred-day moving average and signals a bull trend switching to a bear trend. Conversely, a "golden cross" occurs when an asset's short-term moving average crosses above its long-term moving average. The golden cross most commonly refers to the fifty-day moving average crossing above the two-hundred-day moving average and signals a switch from a bear trend to bull. While these crosses are widely observed on the one-day time frame, a low-frame trader may use lower time frames and shorter period lengths to trade intraday movements.

Some traders swear by the cross signals; however, to date in the crypto markets, particularly with Bitcoin, death crosses and golden crosses have yielded mixed results. Moving average crosses are lagging indicators because it takes time following a trend reversal for the averaged price to turn. In other words, a major trend change is often already underway by the time they appear. Relatedly, on some occasions, the cross signal will occur but after the asset's value has already taken a turn back in the other direction (see Figure 9.2).

Figure 9.2 (tradingview chart)

Figure 9.2 highlights all recent Bitcoin death crosses (red x) and golden crosses (green x) using the fifty-day and two-hundred-day moving averages. The gold line is the 200MA and the blue line is the 50MA. Let's consider how each of these crosses would have played out as an entry. The first (death cross) occurred roughly three months from the 2017 peak but captured the overall remaining two-thirds of the downtrend.

However, if you entered short right at the cross, you would have suffered a rough month where the price bounced back sharply. The second (golden cross) marked a nice entry into the 2019 bull trend. It wasn't the bottom but between the entry at around $5,000 and top at $14,000 who could complain. The third (death cross) occurred on a bounce but midway down a bearish trend at around the $9,000 level. This would have been a decent entry for a swing short but the trend reversed pretty quickly before the next cross. The fourth (golden cross) was a flop. An entry here that was not abandoned swiftly would have resulted in catastrophic losses. The fifth (death cross) appeared after the huge drop from $10,000 to $3,000 at around $7,000. However, it was short-lived and entering short here would have landed you midway through a sharp recovery. Ouch. Finally, the sixth (golden cross) suggests a move upward. However, if you look at the previous crosses occurring so close together, the suggestion is hardly more than indecision in the market. Time will tell whether this cross is the one that makes it out of the chop.

To conclude, the utility of moving averages is appreciated by many traders. I find the cross signals to be useful in that they confirm an existing trend switch through a lagging indicator. The utility for a position trader is particularly apparent, and I have also seen numerous successful traders use the indicator for short time frames and trades. As always, whether you decide to use this indicator is a matter or preference.

Bringing it All Together

You may be asking yourself, how does this all fit together? Before you are various techniques and tools of technical analysis. But, how do you know when to apply them and what to apply? Undoubtedly, this is a lot of new information to take in and commit to memory. The answer is not always so black and white. Successful trades may encompass one or several of the techniques mentioned above. Generally, I look for trades illuminating multiple indicators pointing the same direction. For instance, chart pattern breaks supported by RSI divergences or candlestick reversal formations aligned with trend channels or trend lines (i.e. a gravestone doji confirmed right at a resistance line to enter short). Don't worry if you're confused so far or if you feel like you'll never memorize all of these elements. Like anything, practice makes perfect. You'll get there. Chapter 10 of Part III is specifically designed to further guide you through the application of technical analysis.

III. TRADE STRATEGIES AND THEORY

The final part of the handbook is dedicated to strategies and considerations that are essential to becoming a successful trader. In the first part of the handbook you learned the procedural steps to trading, the second part taught you the technical skills required to trade, and this part will provide you with the strategies and theory required to apply those techniques successfully. Part III first explains proper risk management, offers a strategy to assess trend tops and bottoms, and introduces traders to the evidence-based trading approach with a start-to-finish example. After, I examine different types of crypto markets and market conditions, explore the impact of legacy markets on crypto, and explain fundamental analysis and long-term trade strategies. Finally, I discuss dealing with losing, how to avoid gamblers' mentality, and offer other useful insights catered toward crypto traders.

CHAPTER 10:
ESSENTIAL TRADE STRATEGIES

Applying Risk Management

Risk management is the cornerstone of profitable trading. Every trader is going to be wrong frequently and profits are made by mitigating losses and maximizing winners, which is easier said than done. Through proper risk management: sizing; regularly using stop-losses; executing trades with a disciplined, objective strategy; and being exchange conscious, a trader can protect profits and hard-earned capital.

Size your position appropriately. As a general rule of thumb, you should never risk more than 2-3% of your total capital in a single trade. Every new trader will learn, and every experienced trader has learned, letting losing trades continue in the hope the position will reverse back in your favor can result in quick and ruinous losses. If a trade, and the possibility of it losing, is keeping you up at night that's perhaps a sign you are over-exposed.

Always have a stop-loss in place and have your entry and exit planned before you enter the trade. As a new trader, you will quickly realize the difference between saying "Oh, that's a head and shoulders reversal, I'd short that," and actually taking that position. It's much easier to appear objective when your money is not on the line. Following a rigid stop-loss strategy and practicing discipline with execution can save you from your emotional self, which is generally the self that loses the most money. Regarding stop-loss placement, refer back to the technical analysis section of the handbook where I discuss stop-loss strategy further.

Maintain objectivity. As noted on several occasions in this handbook, having an openness to being wrong and the will to act on it is vital to a trader. Don't let preconceived notions trap you in a bad trade if they turn out to be false! Paradoxically, profitability is often simply achieved through objective execution, however, the equation gets complicated when emotion is involved and that frequently comes as soon as money is on the table. Therefore, adopting strict rules, which I propose in the following sections, is essential to maintaining objectivity.

Moreover, if you are margin trading – don't over leverage! As tempting as it may be to slam the 50x or 100x leverage button on a long because what could possibly go wrong, you are simply gambling and not trading. I rarely exceed 2-5x leverage. There have been some exceptions, but in 95% of situations leveraging above 5x is unnecessary and not in line with my best practice strategy.

Finally, be mindful of where you are trading. If you are trading on a small cap exchange with low liquidity, understand your order could get skipped and may result in losses or missed positions. If you are trading on Bitmex or a high leverage platform, be mindful that these platforms often suffer from slippage and over leveraged positions regularly get liquidated. If you are concerned your position may be subject to an unacceptable loss due to slippage or illiquidity, it may be a sign you are over leveraged or are not on a more reputable exchange.

Calling Tops and Bottoms

Calling an exact top or exact bottom of a trend is an elusive task. Fortunately, it's one a trader does not need to master. Rather, a goal for a trader should be to enter a trend change at the earliest time, which is also supported by a reasonable and substantial chance of success. Remember, the objective of a trader is to *act on a strong inclination that the market will behave a certain way imminently*. This evidence-based approach requires a trader be able to identify indicators with supporting corroboration to prove their mere theory of trend reversal.

Liken calling a trend reversal to a detective investigating a murder: a woman is found dead from a knife wound and foul play is suspected. The detective thinks her husband who has a history of domestic abuse may be involved, but at the moment it's just a theory. In law, before someone is arrested probable cause must be established, which requires evidence beyond a mere suspicion. It's the detective's job to find the weapon, interrogate the suspect, question witnesses, and look at conflicting evidence indicating the man's innocence before arresting him on probable cause. And, even then, the detective still may have the wrong guy.

The same can be applied to trend and pattern analysis. Did the bears just murder the bull and is the trend about to reverse? Ask yourself, do you have probable cause? Is there a confirmed reversal pattern? What time frames does it appear on? Does the volume support the reversal? How heavily does the conflicting divergence on the RSI weigh against the reversal? What other indicators show strength or weakness in the reversal? Only after all considerations establish a reasonable and substantial chance of success supporting your trade theory should a trader consider the reversal.

While it may feel good to nail the top of a wick before a trend reversal, it's likely not a sustainable way to enter a trade. If a trend change or reversal pattern is truly the top or the bottom, a valuable trade will not depend on nailing the exact peak. Ironically, the best time to sell is often when others are piling in, and the best time to buy is often when people are panic selling. The markets like to punish the collective psyche. Therefore, it's essential to look at the technical disposition and not get caught up in the hype.

Adopting Hard Evidence-Based Rules BEFORE Entering a Trade

Every trader should have a list of their own hard rules or guidelines that must be met before entering a trade. Thus, I propose eight rules and evidence-based conditions that must be satisfied before entering any trade: 1) the trade must have a theory; 2) the trade must have a predefined entry and exit; 3) candle formations, chart patterns, trends, or other indicators must be sufficiently developed on large enough time frames;

4) the greater market conditions are assessed; 5) supporting indicators are identified; 6) conflicting indicators are investigated; 7) a judgment is made between the weight of the supporting indicators against the conflicting indicators; and 8) a profit plan is in place and the total acceptable loss is established in case the trade sours. Only after you fulfill these rules and conditions honestly should you enter your trade.

An easy way of satisfying these trade conditions is by going through each one in question form: 1) what is the trade theory; 2) does the trade have a predefined entry and exit; 3) is the pattern or trend sufficiently developed on a large enough time frame(s); 4) what are the market conditions; 5) what supporting indicators exist; 6) what conflicting indicators exist; 7) do the supporting indicators outweigh the negative ones; and 8) what am I willing to risk and where will I take profit?

What is the Trade Theory?

Every trade should have a theory or hypothesis grounded by technical and strategic logic. For example, if you are trading a trend channel, your theory may be the asset has been ranging within a small controlled scope for many months; thus, a departure and break from this tight range will likely mean a sustained move in that direction. It's important to spell out your theory because it keeps traders from entering positions simply based on "chart will go up" or "chart will go down." Like the murder example, trades should be equated to a suspect that you are willing to either book or release based on all of the evidence and incorporating new evidence as it becomes apparent.

Does the Trade Have a Predefined Entry and Exit?

All trades should have a predefined entry and exit. If you enter a trade without a plan on when to get out, you run the risk of panic when the trade goes sour and further increasing losses. These predefined markers should be followed with a strict protocol and be executed objectively without emotion. When your exit or stop gets hits, the trade is over. I caution: DO NOT seek to re-enter the same trade again or you risk succumbing to gamblers' mentality. There will always be another trade. When marking an exit, consider what price shift would invalidate your trade theory.

Is the Pattern or Trend Sufficiently Developed?

All patterns and trends should be sufficiently developed on larger time frames before entering a trade. What type of pattern or trend are you going to trade and how long has it been developing? If it's a pattern, does it exist on multiple time frames (i.e. 2H, 4H, 1D)? How many touches are on the support and resistance lines? Is the pattern fully developed? Does the pattern constitute a continuation generally or a reversal? If you are trading a trend line, how many times has the price touched the line? Is it a well-defined trend line over a long period of time or are you rushing into a weak trend line that only delineates a small bit of price action?

What are the Market Conditions?

Know the market conditions you are trading in. If it's a bear market, understand the burden is on the asset not to paint lower lows and lower highs on the larger time frames and greater chart construction. If it's a bull market, the opposite is true. Consider how long the market has been performing in a bullish or bearish manner and why. Ask yourself, are there fundamental reasons why the market is trading in a downtrend or uptrend and will they affect this trade? Think about what macro-economic events might help sway a market from one trend to another. Could these conditions change quickly or are they likely not going to change anytime soon. While this handbook focuses on the technical analysis, such analysis is not mutually exclusive from the fundamentals and often they coincide. Fundamental analysis is a subject addressed later in Chapter 12 of Part III.

What are the Supporting Indicators?

All supporting technical indicators or lack thereof should be considered. Going back to the example of a policeman investigating a murder, all corroborating evidence should be noted and any deficiency in finding corroborating evidence should also be recognized. What candlesticks support your theory? Does the volume or lack thereof support it? Is the RSI in bull or bear territory? Are there positive divergences? The strength of a trade is best measured when understanding the sum of all the parts.

What are the Conflicting Indicators?

Similarly, all conflicting or negative technical indicators must be identified and considered. It will only hurt your wallet if you choose to ignore powerful conflicting indicators. Are there conflicting candlestick formations? What about divergences moving contrary to your trade theory? Is there a lack of volume? Could there be two potential competing chart patterns in play? Run through all possible negative technical indicators objectively.

Do the Supporting Indicators Outweigh the Conflicting Indicators?

You are the judge and jury of every trade. The scales of financial success are in your hands. Combine the answers to the past two questions and weigh the positive and negative indicators. If there is even a close competition, I'd caution there's probably a better trade on a later day. What you are really looking for, again, is *to act on a strong inclination that the market will behave a certain way imminently.* A trade should look so obvious you would be a fool not to take it. Thus, you limit yourself to only the most promising setups.

What am I Willing to Risk & Where Will I Take Profit?

Finally, how much capital are you willing to risk? This answer should certainly be within the range of your general trade strategy (many traders limit losses on a single trade to 2-3% or less if the trader has a large cash reserve). Your predefined entry and exit should be premeasured to account for the loss you are willing to accept. Similarly, a trader should have some idea of where they will take profit and how. Do you have a specific target or are you going to wait patiently to watch what develops? Will you target multiple levels? Will you set a stop-limit or use a trailing stop? What are your plans to let the trade ride if it goes well? On many occasions, you may not have a strict plan for taking profit because it may require observing chart development. However, you should always have a stop-loss and some realistic idea of how you'd like the successful trade to go.

Trade Example and Rule Analysis in Practice (Short-Frame)

Figure 10.1 (tradingview chart)
The evidence-based trade approach in practice on the 4H chart. A pennant before breakout.

What is the Trade Theory?

In this instance, Bitcoin has made two consecutive bullish moves and has consolidated in a pennant shaped like a symmetrical triangle. My trade theory is an upward break of the pennant would lead to another bullish move where hard resistance would be met around $9,500 (the trend resistance line spanning 10 months if you were to zoom out). If that resistance is broken, a stronger move upward seems probable.

What are the Entry and Exit?

A break above the pennant's resistance line at $9,001 marks the entry and a break below the support line at $8,500 marks the stop-loss.

Is the Pattern or Trend Sufficiently Developed?

The pattern is sufficiently developed on the 2-4H time frames. Three touches on the resistance line and two on the support define the pennant. Notably, this is not a macro level trade, but one based on price action over the past few weeks used as a process example for the handbook.

What are the Market Conditions?

The market conditions are a mixed bag depending on the time frames examined. For the past month Bitcoin has staged a strong recovery after falling from $10,500 to $3,500. On the macro scale, Bitcoin failed to push a higher high on its ten-month downtrend; however, on the shorter time frames, Bitcoin is staging a strong bullish recovery. On the fundamental side, the next Bitcoin halving is approaching, and media is widely hyping this as a positive event.

What are the Supporting Indicators?

A hidden bullish divergence on the RSI supports the theory of trend continuation. Moreover, according to my chart pattern analysis, a bull-biased pennant occurring in a USD(T) paired market signals bullish trend continuation 71.84% of the time. Notably, this pennant is clearly visible on the 4H frame and is small but also visible on the 1D, so I am comfortable using this statistic for this example. Finally, sell volume has also been declining since the local top indicating buyers maintain control.

What are the Conflicting Indicators?

RSI is drooping into bearish territory and was recently very overbought. Bitcoin is not far from long-time trend resistance around $9,500. Bitcoin has also staged a shocking recovery since falling ~70%. This would be a third consecutive bullish advance since the high 6,000s, and I am not sure as we approach resistance if the bulls will run out of steam. I also know from my performance analysis that bull-biased pennants, despite their high continuation frequency, often appear as local tops after several bullish advances.

Do the Supporting Indicators Outweigh the Conflicting Ones?

The bullish continuation pattern coupled with a clear hidden bullish divergence on the RSI and declining sell volume outweigh conflicting indicators, at least until $9,500. The 71.84% odds of a bull-biased pennant breaking upward are strongly in my favor. The RSI moving into bear territory is outweighed by the hidden bullish divergence. Also, the RSI resetting from very overbought conditions should be weighed positively in light of the divergence.

What am I Willing to Risk?

I am willing to risk the spread between the converging support and resistance lines of the pennant (roughly 5%). I will buy .1 bitcoin at $9,001+ for ~$900 for this example trade. Selling at $8,499 for a loss of $50 if the trade fakes out and reverses below the support line.

Target

Ideally, I see this going to $9,500 where I will re-assess. If $9,500 breaks I will watch for a powerful move upward and sell when technical indicators signal reversal.

Trade Development

Figure 10.2 (tradingview chart)
Bitcoin stopped right at trend resistance. No overarching new bearish indicators are present and buy volume is increasing, so I will wait for consolidation and a second attempt. Stop-loss moved to entry.

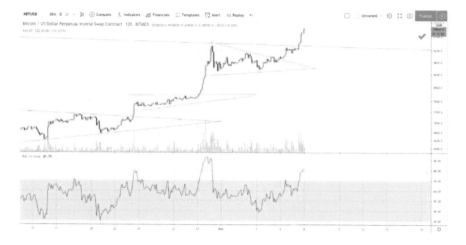

Figure 10.3 (tradingview chart)
Bitcoin broke the resistance line and accelerated upward.

Figure 10.4 (tradingview chart)
Bitcoin made it to $10,000, but, shortly after, a large RSI bearish divergence on the 4H chart appeared spanning from the top of the pennant to the new high. This seems like a good place to exit the trade as a reversal seems imminent.

The Result

Entry: $9,005

Exit: $9,900

STOP-LOSS: $8,499

Win? Yes, the trade was a success. A sell was placed at $9,900 where the RSI divergence on the 4H chart confirmed, which totaled a ~10% gain (no leverage). Not bad for a short-term example trade.

CHAPTER 11:
TRADING ALTCOINS AND
DIFFERENT MARKET CONDITIONS

Trading Altcoins

Crypto offers speculators a wide array of coins and tokens. Any crypto that is not Bitcoin is considered an alternative coin or "altcoin." Yes, in this instance, the term includes both coins and tokens! Today, more than 8,000 altcoins are in circulation. Trading them frequently offers greater volatility than Bitcoin and thus presents traders with an opportunity for greater profit. However, this same volatility also makes trading altcoins riskier as the volatility cuts both ways. If caught on the wrong end, an irresponsible trader may be punished. The next several sections are all about trading altcoins. To do so successfully, traders MUST understand Bitcoin's impact on altcoins and Bitcoin dominance; know the significance and difference between trading the small, medium, and large market cap altcoins; and recognize what it means for profits when you trade an altcoin on a Bitcoin pair vs. a fiat pair. Additionally, following the discussion on altcoins, I discuss the broader impact of the stock markets on Bitcoin, and, consequently, altcoins.

Bitcoin's Impact on Trading Altcoins

The greatest consideration any trader should have when contemplating whether to trade any altcoin whether small, medium, or large cap should be Bitcoin's current effect on the altcoin market. As a trader with half a decade of experience in the crypto markets, I've noticed several distinct patterns that emerge regarding Bitcoin's price movement and its impact on the price movement of the altcoin market. There are four distinct patterns: BTC Up, Alts Up; BTC Up, Alts Down; BTC Down, Alts Down; Bitcoin Down, Alts Up. ***Generally speaking, Bitcoin's impact on the altcoin market is enormous. As a rule of thumb, particularly if I am unsure what correlation is active, I will not buy or long an altcoin if Bitcoin does not also look bullish or stable.*** Additionally, if Bitcoin looks like it will make a power move, I may hold off on altcoins and look to Bitcoin only. For a majority of price action over the past three years, Bitcoin has been the leader and determining factor setting pace.

Bitcoin Up, Alts Up

This correlation means when Bitcoin's price rises so do the altcoins. This is extremely common. Historically, if you look back at the past three years when the altcoin market and Bitcoin market were booming, the largest gainer periods occurred when both Bitcoin and altcoins rose together. This correlation occurs when market sentiment shows trader/investor faith in both Bitcoin and the altcoin market at the same time.

Bitcoin Up, Alts Down

This correlation means that when the price of Bitcoin goes up, the altcoin prices go down. This is also quite common. Why? Because frequently when Bitcoin is going on a bullish tear, traders ditch their altcoin holdings for Bitcoin. Whether because of FOMO ("fear of missing out") or a belief they will be able to better profit or repurchase altcoins at a lower price, on these occasions, traders have successfully grown crypto or cash holdings by playing this scenario strategically.

Bitcoin Down, Alts Down

Painfully common, this correlation means when Bitcoin's price goes down altcoin prices also go down. Bitcoin is the big granddaddy of crypto, and all too often when he suffers, everything else does as well. This scenario is exactly what makes being an altcoin HODLer so painful sometimes.

Bitcoin Down, Alts Up

This is the goldilocks of the correlations for altcoin HODLers and is by far the rarest. In this correlation, when Bitcoin goes down altcoins go up. Why? I'd speculate this occurs when the underlying belief regarding why Bitcoin is going down is considered by market participants to be insignificant. Thus, traders look to increase profit or increase Bitcoin holdings by pumping their Bitcoin in the altcoin market with the belief that the depreciation in Bitcoin's value is only temporary.

Bitcoin Dominance and "Alt Season"

Bitcoin dominance means the percentage of total market capitalization Bitcoin has relative to the entire crypto market capitalization. Interestingly, Bitcoin dominance can be charted, and traders often treat the chart and its patterns, trends, and structure the same as they would with a regular crypto asset. Rather than price on the Y axis, the dominance chart has Bitcoin's percentage of market share (between 0 to 100). When Bitcoin is performing very well, it tends to dominate the market capitalization of the whole space. Exemplified in figure 11.1 below is a chart showcasing Bitcoin dominance. Notice the general trend structures, the RSI divergences signaling trend changes, and how in early 2018 Bitcoin's dominance crashed while the altcoins' market share soared.

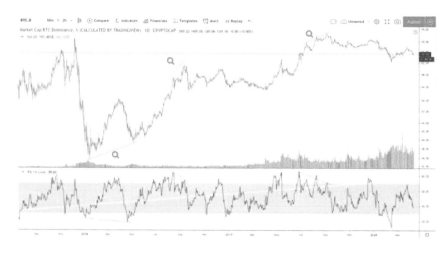

Figure 11.1 RSI Divergences (tradingview chart)

"Alt season," a term coined by traders/HODLers, is a trading period where the altcoin market is on a powerful bullish run. Generally, alt seasons are marked by a noticeable decline in Bitcoin dominance as the altcoins take market share from Bitcoin. Two notable examples being late Spring and Summer of 2017 and December 2017-January 2018. In 2017, the altcoin market exploded from a mere 700 million dollars to 400 billion. While 2017 was a period of massive growth, there were many months of retracement and consolidation for altcoins (some retracing as much as 80% against Bitcoin). Thus, it should be distinguished as being two alt seasons rather than one. As highlighted below, these alt seasons were marked by an obvious decline in Bitcoin dominance.

Alt seasons may begin under different circumstances. In early 2017, it began with an overall bullish momentum for all cryptos including Bitcoin. The majors like Bitcoin and Ethereum led the pack. Late 2016 was a low period in crypto, and Ethereum which had reached nearly $30 months earlier was down to just $5. Slowly, everything appeared to rise from the ashes together, and, by May 2017, a price exploration began as Bitcoin reclaimed its all-time high. Altcoins quickly outpaced Bitcoin and melted its dominance into the summer. Some cryptos logged 1,000-20,000%+ gains. In other words, life-changing gains.

The late 2017 alt season and bubble peak commenced differently. While many altcoins shed a significant portion of new-found value between late summer and fall, Bitcoin continued a steadier bullish trajectory. Bitcoin dominance increased from 50% back to 70% as altcoiners abandoned their coin to capitalize on the Bitcoin euphoria. However, when Bitcoin started to show signs of weakening and altcoin/BTC pairs were heavily dumped and oversold by weak hands, the Bitcoin piled back into the altcoin market. Interestingly, the 2017 high for Bitcoin peaked in mid-December, which is where the altcoin run truly began and moved quickly for another month.

Figure 11.2 Tickers: BTC.D & TOTAL2 (tradingview charts)
The chart on top shows Bitcoin's dominance melting away from 95% in early 2017 to just 36% by the end of 2017. Notice the recovery of Bitcoin dominance between alt seasons where altcoins paired against Bitcoin had a significant retrace and Bitcoin dominance recovered from 50% back to 70%.

Correspondingly, below, the altcoin market capitalization displays the meteoric rise of altcoins during the 2017/early 2018 alt seasons.

Unfortunately, both of these charts now show large gaps likely because of tweaks to the data aggregation.

Performance Analysis Findings Related to Bitcoin Dominance and Altcoins

Several interesting findings surfaced from the performance analysis of chart patterns that shed additional light on the relationship between Bitcoin and altcoins. First, several patterns tended to appear dominantly in one category of pairings over the other. Second, cryptos trading against USD(T) tended to have a higher degree of volatility.

Unexpectedly, bear flags appeared more frequently in BTC traded pairs than USD(T) pairs, while bull flags appeared more frequently in USD(T) pairs (BTC pairs comprised 56% of all sampled bear flags and only 40% of all sampled bull flags). Relatedly, ascending triangles appeared twice as frequently in USD(T) traded pairs. Why? I'd speculate the direct relationship of Bitcoin on altcoins played a role here. To elaborate, think about times where Bitcoin is going up and altcoins are being driven down. For example, in Winter 2017. In November and December 2017, alt/BTC pairs like Ethereum were painting bear flags while their USD(T) pairs were painting bull flags. This happened because holders were selling Ethereum for Bitcoin, but Bitcoin was rising quickly and the USD value of Ethereum was still rising despite the sell-off of the BTC pairs. Speculators continued to pour money into Ethereum with fiat, offsetting those selling into Bitcoin. This accounts for both an additional bear flag in the BTC pair record and an additional bull flag in the USD(T) record from only one crypto. Thus, it's likely this scenario played out similarly with other pairs and in other in times when BTC and USD(T) values were divergent. In other instances, if an alt/BTC pair was trading mostly flat but Bitcoin was rising against the dollar, alt/USD(T) pairs would share similar pattern formation as BTC/USD(T). So, this may also account for instances where more bull flags appear in USD(T) related pairs.

Relatedly, USD(T) pairs across the board exhibited higher performance volatility, both going up and down for nearly every pattern examined in the chart pattern study. Why? Think about it: during a period where Bitcoin is going down against the dollar and alt/BTC pairs are also going down, the losses are going to be compounded in the USD(T) pairings. Conversely, in periods where altcoins are rising against BTC while

Bitcoin is rising against the dollar, the gains are also going to be compounding but upward. So, if an alt/BTC pair has a bull flag at the same time as Bitcoin is trending upward, the gains are amplified and the altcoin enjoys both the rise against Bitcoin and Bitcoin's rise against the dollar.

Trading Small Caps vs. Large Caps

With thousands of coins and tokens traded publicly every day, the variance in market capitalizations (the total value of an asset's coins or tokens in circulation) is extreme. Some of the major cryptos like Bitcoin or Ethereum have a market cap in the tens of billions of dollars, while thousands of tiny start-up companies have market caps in the hundreds of thousands or several million-dollar range. Others, the midcaps, have something in between ranging from the hundreds of millions to a billion-dollar category. Overall, trading different cap coins is a matter of preference with many traders feeling strongly about what range (small, medium, or large cap) they trade. Trading the different market caps can all be profitable but may require different approaches and might not suit all trading styles or goals.

The smaller the market cap, the less money it takes to move the asset price up or down. For example, say a small cap company launched an ICO with 10,000,000 tokens circulating. Each token is currently priced at $.02 creating a $200,000 market capitalization. Thus, at the current price of .02/token, the entire supply could be bought for $200,000. Assume 1,000 ICO participants hold the tokens and the current price reflects the ICO sales price. It's fair to say the entire supply would not be up for sale at base price with so many holders. Consequently, if a buyer comes in with $20,000 to invest in the token, which would account for 10% of the entire supply at the price of .02/token, it's very likely that buyer would move the value of the token up easily with that $20,000. Conversely, say Ethereum is trading at $150 with a supply of one hundred and ten billion coins, its market capitalization would amount to sixteen billion dollars. If a trader comes in with $20,000 or even $200,000 it would barely make a dent in the current price – assuming regular liquidity exists on the exchange.

Some traders enjoy trading small cap coins because they often have large price swings due to small market capitalization and low liquidity. It's not uncommon to see small cap coins move 20%, 30%, or even 100% in a single day. But traders should note these price fluctuations swing both ways. Overnight, profit takers can dump a small cap coin back down to where it started or below.

Other traders may prefer only to trade the largest cap coins with the most liquidity to fill big orders and ensure their orders don't get skipped. Completely understandable if you are a margin trader or are playing with large amounts of money. Certainly, something can also be said about lowering risk by only playing the larger caps, as smaller cap coins have a greater reputation for being scams and may be subject to more scrutiny from regulators.

The application of technical analysis on large caps vs. small caps is debatable. I have heard doubt from many traders on the applicability of technical analysis to small caps because of the ability for relatively small amounts of money to push an asset out of the realm of normal price action activity. While in some instances this is true, I think in many cases technical analysis is applicable to small cap coins. I have traded many small caps with similar success to large caps using candlestick formations, chart patterns, trend lines, and divergences.

Showcased in Figure 11.3 and Figure 11.4 below is the COTI/BTC pair in February 2020. COTI, a small cap under $3,000,000 USD at entry, was consolidating as a symmetrical triangle over several weeks. Huge volume created a stir of volatility creating a bottom from a protracted decline. The triangle ended up busting out and surfing the trend line for a little while before charging a strong reversal and netting a whopping 200%+ gain. A nice low cap swing trade with relatively clean and successful pattern analysis. Notably, a stop-loss was placed below the support line.

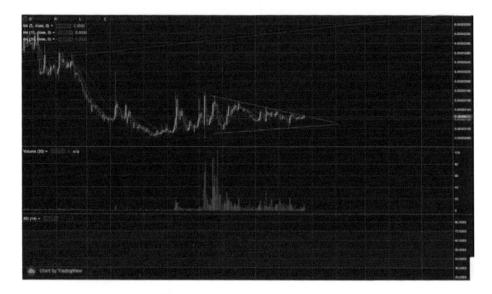

Figure 11.3 COTI/BTC, 1D, 2020, Kucoin
This chart highlights a clean small-cap symmetrical triangle before breakout.

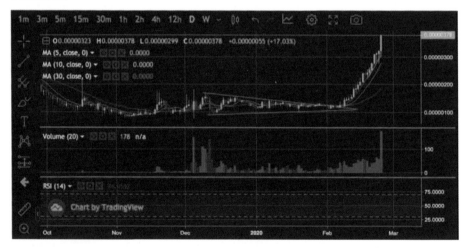

Figure 11.4 COTI/BTC, 1D, 2020, Kucoin
Here, COTI broke upward more than doubling against Bitcoin in just a few weeks.

Below Figure 11.5 shows another example of a clean micro-cap (MWAT/BTC) trade from 2018. Notice a bubble-like run-up followed by a five-month burst and decline with lower lows and lower highs. It's similar to a falling wedge or a descending trend channel but doesn't quite fit the trend lines. Still, trading the overall trend break resulted in a near

100% gain and 63% in a mere day.

Figure 11.5 MWAT/BTC, 1D, 2018, Kucoin
These charts show the before and after pop of a descending and controlled deflation, which nearly resembles a falling wedge or a descending trend channel with lower highs and lower lows.

Trading for Bitcoin vs. Trading for Fiat

One novel nuance of crypto trading as opposed to other markets is traders may be speculating with a goal to either cash out into fiat currencies or others may trade with the ambition to accumulate more Bitcoin. Keep in mind, many altcoins are only paired with Bitcoin and only the more liquid ones have a fiat pair. Many traders see altcoin trading as an opportunity to grow their Bitcoin stack, and many Bitcoin enthusiasts value Bitcoin more than fiat currencies.

This can lead to some confusion, particularly in periods when altcoins are rising against Bitcoin but Bitcoin's value in dollars is going down. Some traders measure a trade's success as an altcoin's percentage gain relative to Bitcoin rather than the altcoin's value in dollars or other fiat. This is confusing because you may have a day when say Ethereum rises 10% against Bitcoin, but Bitcoin falls 12%+ against the dollar. Technically, Ethereum will also have gone down in dollars but substantially up in Bitcoin. One trader may say this is a great success because they made 10% more Bitcoin, while another trader may say this is a failure because they lost value in dollars. The inverse is true as well. For example, Ethereum may fall 5% against Bitcoin but Bitcoin may gain 10% against the dollar. Thus, a trader may say "down in Bitcoin, up in dollars."

Ultimately, it's a matter of preference. I tend to think that only fiat pays the bills and trade with the primary goal of accumulating stable coins or dollars. Others disagree. The important thing to understand is altcoin trading is done largely against Bitcoin, and, if you want to secure profits in fiat (if no fiat or stable coin pair exists), you may need to execute two trades: the first to sell the altcoin for Bitcoin and the second to sell the Bitcoin into a stable coin or fiat currency.

The Impact of Legacy Markets on Crypto

In addition to Bitcoin's performance and dominance impacting the greater crypto space, traders should also be mindful of what, if any, relationship or influence legacy markets (i.e. major stock indexes) have on the current crypto market. Often crypto appears to act independently, particularly because no other market in the world has so much consistent volatility. However, evidence supports the argument that crypto is an asset class that performs best under bullish conditions in the global markets. For instance, take the epic 2017 crypto bull run, which occurred during a steep rise in a 10-year equities bull run. I am certainly not the first or only one to note this observation.

An easy comparison shows Bitcoin, and thus crypto, often coincides with the S&P 500. If you take a chart comparing Bitcoin with the S&P 500 (see Figure 11.6), you can see most of the major Bitcoin dumps coincided with negative volatility in the S&P 500. In other words, when the S&P 500 dipped or dumped, Bitcoin often did too and repeatedly with greater thrust. However, this is not to say Bitcoin is always performing concurrently with the S&P 500. In 2018, the stock markets performed substantially better than Bitcoin did, but both ended that year with a big dump.

Notably, since the coronavirus started impacting the legacy markets, Bitcoin shares a striking correlation with the S&P 500 down to even the low frame charts, but, again, with greater volatility. Many crypto-enthusiasts would like to argue Bitcoin (and crypto), born from the folly of the 2008 financial crisis, was designed for this instance and acts independently. However, with such a striking correlation to the legacy markets, whether Bitcoin becomes a hedge to the greater financial markets has yet to be proven. Still, with governments printing seemingly unlimited amounts of rescue cash and recession looming, perhaps 2020 will be the year the markets truly diverge and Bitcoin becomes a global hedge. We'll see!

Figure 11.6 S&P 500 Futures and BTC/USD (tradingview chart)
Notice how often a big Bitcoin (orange) crash or dip coincided with a dump or dip in the S&P 500 (red candles).

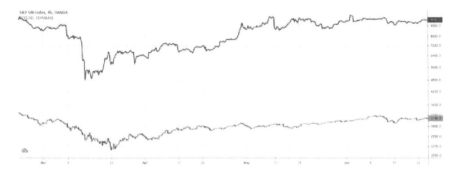

Figure 11.7 S&P 500 Futures and BTC/USD (tradingview chart)
This 4H chart shows a clear correlation between Bitcoin (orange) and the S&P 500 following the initial coronavirus dump. Bitcoin appears to follow closely while also exhibiting greater volatility. This may be in part because margin trading liquidations fuel greater spikes and dips in the crypto markets, as they are far less liquid than the S&P 500.

No doubt, one of the big challenges of trading crypto is keeping tabs on all of the moving parts and interrelationships. Already I have discussed Bitcon's various impacts on the market, the interaction between USD(T) and BTC pairs, and now the legacy market influences. Understandably, it can make one's head spin. Unfortunately, no easy fix exists to detangle it all and traders simply need to be observant of multiple factors at any given time.

CHAPTER 12:
LONG-TERM STRATEGIES

Fundamental Analysis

You may hear traders or HODLers use the term fundamental analysis or "FA." Fundamental analysis means studying, measuring, and predicting the value of an asset based on the intrinsic or "fundamental" aspects of an asset. For example, the cost of production, adoption of the asset, number of users, growth of users, development of the technology, war chest of the team, caliber of developers, or any other metric seeking the asset's inherent rather than price-action-based value. To illustrate, Bitcoin requires an enormous amount of electricity for miners to create a single new coin. If the cost of production for a single bitcoin is $5,000 for miners with a very low electricity price rate, then traders or investors applying fundamental analysis may argue the intrinsic value of a single bitcoin is not lower than the lowest cost of production ($5,000).

Numerous crypto trading groups exist where the focus of when to buy and sell a crypto is based on the fundamentals rather than the technical aspects. Traders in these groups may call themselves "gem hunters" or "fundamental analysts." Rather than analyzing the charts, they scrutinize the technology, teams and developers, marketing strategies, communities, and other aspects of the asset. Rather than seeking a technical indicator flashing a buy signal, these traders may simply look for any market dip as opportunities to buy. Communications like press releases indicating big news from the delivering team frequently signal fundamental-based entries.

Crypto traders are often split between the two camps of fundamental and technical analysts. The steadfast HODLers often fall under the fundamental analyst category because they subscribe to the belief that regardless of the market movements in the near future, the technological achievement and use of the crypto will drive its value to a higher price in the future. Many traders often subscribe to the technical analysis camp because it allows them greater latitude to speculate on the short, medium, and long-term price of an asset grounded by repeating market behaviors. Still, both philosophies share significant crossover in membership, and the more open-minded market participants from each camp often complement each other nicely when sharing theories on crypto asset values.

Consider the recent Bitcoin halving as an example. The fundamental analysis camp argued Bitcoin's value should go up because block rewards (the amount of bitcoin mined in each block) reduced by 50%. Thus, it became twice as costly to produce a single bitcoin. Meanwhile the technical analysis camp could easily recognize the preceding appreciation of Bitcoin's value leading to the havening event. Moreover, the technical camp could quantify the recent price action and offer insights into volume, trend structure, and potential points of resistance or weakness. In this instance, both camps could offer complimentary material supporting a theory that Bitcoin's value would rise near the halving.

As highlighted, technical analysis and fundamental analysis are not mutually exclusive and can be applied together to create two lines of attack for speculators. I suggest all traders consider potential fundamental influences on the assets they trade, regardless of whether you subscribe heavily to one belief over the other. In the same vein, if you are a HODLer and not a trader, I suggest you consider how technical analysis might bolster your entries and exits next time you are looking to time the market. Avoid becoming a HODLer who takes every unmitigated market blow when it can be avoided.

Hedging

A hedge is a strategic trade used to counterbalance ("hedge") losses from a short-term reversal while a trader holds open a position(s). For instance, in some circumstances, a trader may wish to hedge a trade in the opposite direction of their primary trade to secure or maximize profit. To extrapolate hypothetically, say I bought two spot-market bitcoins near a recent bottom at $4,000 each. Bitcoin is now trading at $7,500. I am anticipating taking this position for several months with a target of $15,000, but in the near term I see an immediate retrace in price to the $5,000 area. I don't want to sell my spot bitcoins, which requires moving them from cold storage and potentially losing my position. But I also don't want to lose my profit. So, I hedge an opposing short with a stop-loss above the recent high and target in the low $5,000s. I can close the trade when I see bullish indicators return. If it turns out I was wrong to think Bitcoin would keep going to $15,000 and it becomes clear $7,500 was the top, my hedge position will help reduce my lost profit as Bitcoin declines before I sell. I could even keep it open after I sell the bitcoins and turn the hedge into a profitable primary short.

Balancing hedge sizing will take some practice. I generally do a low leverage counter-position at 2-5x leverage. My hedges do not cover the full size of the entire open position but seek to cover a large portion (30-50%). So, in the example above, I might take $2,000 and leverage it to be worth $5,000 (33% of my two bitcoins currently worth $15,000) as a short, which will appreciate as Bitcoin retraces.

Hedging is popular for long-term investors who don't want to trade frequently and believe in the long-term trend of the assets they are holding. This not only mitigates losses and maximizes profit but also provides longer-term holders with peace of mind during protracted bear trends or in times when a large reversal seems imminent. Still, swing or position traders may also reap the benefits of a hedge and also enjoy the peace of mind. It's not uncommon to see crypto traders hedge short against their altcoin exposure.

Averaging Down

Averaging down is a strategy where a trader or investor buys into an asset at predetermined intervals knowing they will not likely catch the bottom on the first try. By averaging the entry, a trader does not need to find the exact bottom and can average losses and turn them into gains quickly. For example, say Bitcoin peaked last year at $10,000 and it's now sitting at $3,000 after many months of decline. You are confident the bottom is near, but you aren't quite sure where it is. You could average your entry by purchasing first at $3,000 and with the expectation and intention to purchase again at $2,000 and $1,000, if it ever gets to either of those levels. This strategy ensures you are not left in the dust with no holding if Bitcoin has bottomed but also anticipates you may be wrong. If you buy one bitcoin at each level and Bitcoin bottoms at $1,900, you will have bought two bitcoins with an average entry of $2,500 (the mean of 2,000 and 3,000). Thus, you will start to profit when Bitcoin trades above $2,500.

Deciding intervals and position sizing is a matter of personal taste. When I average into a position, I generally plan on three purchases with each larger than the last. I generally expect my first purchase will not be the only one, so I assume I will get more bang for my buck cheaper. Still, I make sure my first purchase is one that I would be happy with if I nailed the bottom. Generally, I place a bid 30-50% lower than my first entry and my second bid 30-50% lower than the first average down. These are not hard rules, and I determine the best course of action based on the particular asset and the totality of the circumstances. I never average into a chart that is not already in a very low period.

Relatedly, investors may choose to regularly purchase an asset to average into a position, which is called Dollar Cost Averaging (DCA). For instance, on a bi-weekly or monthly basis. This strategy is better tailored toward investors rather than traders because it's based on a time-table strategy rather than a price action strategy. Nevertheless, traders should be aware of it and its utility for long-term holdings.

CHAPTER 13:
ADDITIONAL TOOLS AND INSIGHTS
TO HELP YOU MASTER YOUR CRAFT

Where and How to Practice Without Risking Money as a Beginner

No new trader should begin trading with real money. Period. I wouldn't suggest anyone risk any capital trading for at least six months from starting to learn and mastering the core concepts. Fortunately, resources exist to help new traders test the waters!

First, you can familiarize yourself on Tradingview and begin to chart on day one. You can even use markers on any Tradingview chart to delineate where you would enter or exit a position. This is a fun way to hypothetically trade, and even after years of successful trading, I still do this when I'm fairly certain but not convinced enough to make an actual trade. Tradingview also lets you publish your potential positions and look at setups posted by thousands of other traders.

Second, with a slight caveat, Bitmex.testnet is a free service for anyone in the world to try trading using the Bitmex platform. It uses fake bitcoins and you can even be from the United States because it does not involve real assets. This is an excellent resource for learning how to enter and exit a trade. You can practice stop-limit trading, stop-losses, trailing stops, and a variety of other trade mechanisms. Bitmex is also where you can practice longing, shorting, futures, as well as leverage trading with multiple cryptos. However, I suggest new traders only use Bitmex.testnet to practice trade execution techniques. After you enter your practice trades and set a stop-loss, leave the exchange and use a Bitmex chart on Tradingview to follow your testnet position. Sitting on Bitmex and watching the order books flicker like slot machines is a terrible way to learn to trade.

Applying These Trading Techniques to Other Markets

Overall, the same principles of technical analysis can be applied to any market. A trader who understands candlestick formations, chart patterns, trend analysis, or the RSI can apply and test their knowledge on stocks, forex, cryptocurrencies, and commodities. One of the neat things about technical analysis and market behavior is that markets tend to behave in similar ways across the board and the techniques are thus broadly applicable.

But I will caution before you go around telling all your friends you read this book and can trade any market, all markets have their nuances or differences and trading techniques described here are far more developed, studied, and applied in other markets. For instance, candlestick formations and chart patterns have a long history. Traders, mathematicians, and academics have spent decades testing and running statistical analysis and other tests on occurrences and probabilities. If you are trading the stock markets, you should probably use the statistics and insights of Bulkowski or another revered stock trader.

This handbook just gives a thorough but cursory overview and interpretation of some of the most popular patterns and signals, and their appearance and previous applicability in the crypto markets. This is just the very tip of the iceberg, and by no means is it all inclusive. In fact, I hope my readers use this handbook as a stepping stone to further explore the world of trading and technical analysis. This handbook will not make you an expert, but it can give you legs to stand on as you journey into the vast world of trading. As the crypto markets mature over the coming years, we will have more data to apply to crypto-centric trading.

Develop Your Own Strategies

I've never come across two traders who trade exactly the same way. Often traders share similarities in tactics, indicators they use, and pattern analysis. Yet, frequently, two traders look at the exact same chart data and come up with entirely different theories. In fact, if they didn't, and everyone saw markets going the exact same way, we wouldn't have chart analysis or market participants betting against each other. This is all to say, there's no magic key to trading successfully and different traders find success using different methods.

The teachings of this handbook comprise only a single methodology using only a tiny fraction of the available collective knowledge and resources. Some traders don't use pattern analysis but use price action levels, while others look at things like Fibonacci lines or moving averages for key levels of support and resistance. It's up to you to find what works and what doesn't. I hope to get new traders fluent in chart reading, comfortable with the ebb and flow of price action and common trade techniques, and provide the strategic tool belt necessary to manage risk and trade profitably. Beyond this, I hope all traders refine and develop their own successful strategies and techniques.

Gamblers' Mentality: Identification, Prevention, and Mitigation

No proud trader wants to admit it, but on one occasion or another every trader experiences gamblers' mentality. It's practically a rite of passage, but the true rite of passage is identifying the issue and outgrowing it, and quickly. Gamblers' mentality occurs when a trader deviates from a strict, disciplined strategy to embark on a higher risk higher reward trade(s). A trader may try to justify the occasion in their mind by thinking something like the setup merits high leverage and high exposure and that it's not such a big deal.

What are signs of gamblers' mentality? Increasing leverage or increasing position size beyond your normal conservative range, fanciful thoughts of big winnings quickly, quickly re-entering a position after exiting at a loss, over trading to reclaim a recent loss, switching positions from short to long multiple times in a short period of time. One sure sign of gamblers' mentality is your inner monologue convincing you what you are doing is NOT gamblers' mentality.

What can prevent or mitigate gamblers' mentality? Identifying the signs and acting on them is the best course of action. The best mitigation is prevention, which means enforcing hard rules like if you lose a trade you step away from the charts for a day. Often, even having time away from looking at a chart can help you regain objectivity and calm the dopamine receptors. Gamblers' mentality is like a bad dream that you fall back into, and the only way to avoid it is waking up. You must completely wake yourself to ensure you don't fall right back asleep into the same dream. *Take a walk and start a twenty-four hour no trade cooling period.*

If you find yourself breaking the rules and engaging in any gamblers' mentality behavior, have your pre-determined trade rule list to consult. Before going any further, answer all of your hard rules honestly. If any of the rules and considerations are violated, do not engage in the trade and assume you have succumbed to gamblers' mentality.

It's Okay to Be Wrong

Accepting that it's okay to be wrong cannot be overstated. Every trader is going to be wrong on many occasions. The important thing is to manage your trades so that when you are wrong you lose little and when you are right you win big. If you marry your ego to a trade because you have a burning desire to be right, you are going to lose money and look stupid. Sticking with a losing trade because you made a call that the price is going to go down and it goes up, is a terrible thing to do. A good trader should be willing to accept they are wrong and cut losses quickly. Price action is dynamic and charts are frequently evolving. What may have been a good call yesterday may be a bad call today and a bad call today may be a good call tomorrow. Follow the evidence and be able to quickly let loose the trades you misidentified.

How to Move Past a Losing Trade or a Winner You Let Go Too Early

Many traders present themselves online as flawless and always scoring big on every price movement. This can give a novice trader a false sense of what successful trading looks like. The reality is, traders only need to be right a simple majority of the time so long as risk management is properly executed. Many great traders are often wrong. Successful trading is less about being right all the time and more about keeping good trades and ditching bad ones quickly. This section of the handbook is by far the most expensive, and I've suffered many painful losses before being able to write about it. I hope it will cost you less than it cost me when you write retrospectively.

All traders experience painful losers. So, what do we do when we are confronted with one? First, each loss is a learning experience, and you should analyze what went wrong and to the extent possible commit what went wrong to memory so it does not occur again in the future. Consider why your trade failed, what could have prevented it, and how you might approach a similar situation in the future. My trading strategy was built on a foundation of mistakes and losses and was built brick by brick through admitting errors and applying corrections. Second, take a breath and try not to dwell on the recent loser. Of course, it will be a sensitive spot for a while, but keep in mind even successful traders lose frequently. I often take a walk outside after taking a loss to refresh my mind and channeling some of the frustration into exercise can help regain objectivity. I wish I could tell you some trades won't haunt you after you make a mistake, but you are haunted only insofar as you allow yourself to be. Remember your strategy depends overall on having your winners outperform your losers, and you trade with the expectation that not all trades will go your way. Lastly, understand your mentality becomes more durable over time. After several painful burns, you become more familiar with the process and how to grow from it. The emotional ability to handle losses calices like a hand does when learning to play the guitar or the foot of a kick boxer. There's no easy way to earn those calices, which require shredding some sashimi-like flesh.

Something less spoken about but equally important, is mentally dealing with a profitable trade that was exited too early. Many people consider any winning trade as a good one, which is true. However, as many crypto traders can tell you, little stings worse than closing a trade at 20% when it went another 300%. Here's the fact, you are going to make misjudgments and some are heavier than others. We do not know for certain how markets will act in the future, and traders act on what they believe is likely to happen in the foreseeable future. If you take any position in a given day and then reverse course and take the opposite one (not a strategy I endorse generally), one of your decisions would end up having been right. Get the "woulda, coulda, shoulda" attitude out of your head and deal with things as they are. You could always have done better but, in the same vein, you could always have done much worse. In these cases, you did turn a profit! You will have many days where just turning a profit would be refreshing. It's going to be painful along the way, but find solace in the fact that every trader who has any substantial experience shares similar experiences and pain.

You are going to miss trades, misjudge trades, lose trades, and lose profit. Regardless of what stung you, there will always be another trade. There's nothing wrong with taking a step back to regain objectivity and a calm state of mind. It's also okay to let yourself feel the pain. Don't wallow in it, but recognize "wow, that really stings, what can I do to avoid this in the future?" Moreover, don't throw gasoline on the fire. If you sense you are succumbing to any of the signs of gamblers' mentality stop yourself and cool off for at least a 24-hour period.

Tune Out the Logical Fallacies and Hyperbolic Media

Ignore logical fallacies and clickbait headlines from major crypto news sources and influencers. It's important to be able to filter out the noise as a trader and maintain objectivity. Many "shills" and news sources regularly pump garbage news into the space and often make correlations that can harm or confuse a new trader. For example, a few common examples are "every April Bitcoin performs well, so it will here too," "people always sell crypto at Christmas," "every year around the X Convention Bitcoin rises," or "Bitcoin bounces every time it hits this (insert indicator or level)." These amount to nothing more than logical fallacies, which, even if true, do not prove a future event. Correlation does not equal causation. Fallacies are frequently incorrect, and the technical disposition from one occurrence may be vastly different the next time around.

Similarly, every trader following crypto news or finance news will see and articles like "Bitcoin's Crashing" or "Will Bitcoin Survive?" or "Bitcoin is Headed to All Time High." Often news sources fill the headlines with hyperboles and may call a relatively tame move "catastrophic" or "incredible." These news sources are solely after clicks and will sap as many people to their sites as possible through whatever means necessary. Unfortunately, some of the bigger players in crypto media are the biggest offenders. Traders should not engage in trades or lose objectivity because of a media publication describing price action. Again, consult the chart yourself.

This is not to say do not following media, influencers, or traders but merely be able to recognize propaganda when you see it. On other occasions, there may be real news events that affect the markets. For example, regulatory actions, hacks, lawsuits, major global events like pandemics, etc. Macro events certainly can play a role on crypto assets and quickly. Several notable spikes and drops have occurred as a knee-jerk reaction to some significant event. Moreover, I do urge traders to follow other traders – not to copy trades – but to see how different people viewing the exact same data come to different conclusions. I suggest traders keep an open mind when following social media of other traders because if you fill your feeds with an echo chamber, you may miss something important that other people pick up. Also, you may see other traders use different techniques with success and experiment or expand your own strategy. Of course, it's also always fun to see who you are betting against.

Closing Remarks

Congratulations on finishing the Chart Logic handbook! By now, you should have sufficient information to begin or expand your journey trading cryptocurrencies. These techniques and strategies are your key to outperforming your average HODLer. With this knowledge, fear not the price swings and volatility of crypto. Each major movement provides opportunity for those willing to tackle the charts in a disciplined and objective manner. Use the evidence-based approach for each trade to corroborate or dispel your theories profitably. Practice, fail, and then continue practicing. Don't give up, and set your expectations reasonably. Ultimately, success trading is in your hands, and those who dedicate themselves to the craft are rewarded. Best wishes and good luck!

Definitions Key

Altcoin – Any crypto that is not Bitcoin.

Alt Season – A period of time where altcoin prices rise significantly relative to Bitcoin and Bitcoin dominance falls.

Ascending Triangle – A triangle chart pattern with higher lows and a flat or nearly flat top formed over 21 or more days.

Averaging Down – Strategically buying at predetermined levels knowing you likely won't catch the bottom on the first try.

Bearish Divergence – When an asset's price makes a higher high(s) but the oscillator makes a lower high(s) (suggests reversal).

Bear Flag – A flag-shaped chart pattern with a downtrend preceding a rectangular or parallelogram consolidation.

Bear Pennant – A short-term chart pattern formed under 21 days with a preceding downtrend (pole) and consolidation period shaped like a triangle or wedge.

Bid – The price (order) a buyer wishes to purchase an asset at.

Bitcoin Dominance – Bitcoin's market cap % relative to the entire crypto market cap.

Bounce – A temporary positive trend reversal occurring in a downtrend.

Breakdown – When an asset's price breaks below a support line.

Breakout – When an asset's price breaks above a resistance line.

Broadening Wedges – A class of chart patterns with support and resistance lines that fan outward in an ascending, descending, or symmetrical manner.

Bullish Divergence – When the price of an asset prints a lower low(s) while the oscillator displays higher low(s) (suggests bullish reversal).

Bull Flag – A flag-shaped chart pattern with an uptrend preceding a rectangular or parallelogram consolidation.

Bull Pennant – A short-term chart pattern formed under 21 days with a preceding uptrend (pole) and consolidation period shaped like a triangle or wedge.

Buy – To purchase and possess an asset.

Buy Wall – A large bid visible on the order book.

Candle – The price change of an asset over a select period of time (open and close) delineated in a red or green stick.

Candle Body – The solid colored space between the open and close of a candle, which is colored green if price action is positive from open or red if price action is negative from open.

Candle Wick –A thin line representing the high and low of an asset's price during an examined a period before the price changed course. The wick represents the part of the candle that is not the solid portion between the open and close.

Candlestick Formations – Candlestick arrangements suggesting a reversal, consolidation, or continuation. Candlestick formations show the power struggle between buyers and sellers and are frequently used for timing reversals.

Chart – A display of an asset's value over time on X and Y axes.

Chart Patterns – Repeating patterns of price action found in markets that suggest a continuation or reversal in trend.

Circulating Supply – The amount of a crypto circulating that can be traded on exchanges.

Coin – The native currency of a blockchain that can be either mined or pre-mined.

Cold Storage – A secure offline hardware device similar to a USB but designed for security and used to store crypto wallets (private and public keys).

Consolidation – A period where an asset's price moves in a narrow range (consolidates) following a move upward or downward.

Correction – A temporary price decline following an upward move.

Day Trader – A short-term trader who generally closes their positions by the end of each day.

Death Cross – A sell signal occurring when the short-term moving average crosses below the long-term moving average. Frequently this refers to the 50-day and 200-day moving averages.

Descending Triangle – A triangle chart pattern with lower highs and a flat or nearly flat support line formed over 21 or more days.

DEX – A decentralized exchange.

Dollar Cost Averaging (DCA) – Making regular, time-based, purchases of an asset to average an entry.

Double Bottom – A reversal chart pattern appearing after a downtrend and marked by two distinct lows at or nearly at the same level with a failed rally in between.

Double Top – A reversal chart pattern appearing after an uptrend and marked by two distinct highs at or nearly at the same level with a valley in between.

Dump – When an asset is sold off heavily, sharply dropping the value.

Exchange – A platform like a broker where cryptos are bought and sold.

Fakeout – A false breakout or breakdown.

Fiat Currency – A currency issued by a national government (i.c. dollars, euros, pounds, yen, yuan, etc.).

Fundamental Analysis – Assessing the intrinsic value of an asset through evaluation outside of price action analysis.

Gap – An empty space between candles, usually between trading periods, where no asset was bought or sold. Generally, with some exceptions, many crypto charts do not include gaps because the markets are perpetual.

Golden Cross – A buy signal occurring when the short-term moving average crosses above the long-term moving average. Frequently this refers to the 50-day and 200-day moving averages.

Head and Shoulders Pattern – A bearish reversal pattern marked by three consecutive highs with the middle one being highest. The other two similarly lower highs surrounding the highest high create the appearance of a head and two shoulders.

Hedge – A counterbalance trade opposing an existing position to minimize losses and maximize profit.

Hidden Bearish Divergence – When an assets price makes a lower high(s) but the oscillator makes a higher high(s) (suggests bearish continuation).

Hidden Bullish Divergence – When an assets price makes a higher low but an oscillator makes a lower low (suggests bullish continuation).

Hidden Order – An order hidden from the public order book by the buyer or seller, which can be used to accumulate or unload an asset without letting other traders know.

HODL – To hold cryptos for the long-term.

Inverted Head and Shoulders Pattern – A bullish reversal pattern marked by three consecutive lows with the middle one being lowest and two surrounding similarly higher lows creating the appearance of an inverted head and two shoulders.

Large Cap – An altcoin with a large capitalization – generally in the billions of dollars range.

Limit Order – A standard buy or sell order where you set a specific bid or offer price.

Liquidity/Liquid Markets – The ability of a market to have assets change hands without substantially affecting the price. For example, a market with substantial buyers, sellers, and market makers such that a trader can sell/buy a reasonable quantity of an asset without affecting the price greatly is considered liquid. An opposing example would be considered an illiquid market.

Log Scale – The logarithmic chart scale that best portrays exponential growth.

Long – To buy or bet in favor of an asset's price rise with an expectation of profit.

Margin – The amount of funds, used as collateral, necessary to open or keep open a leveraged trade.

Margin Trading – Trading using funds that are borrowed to increase position size beyond what a trader could normally afford.

Market Capitalization – The total value of an asset's entire circulating supply.

Market Order – An order that executes a buy or sell at the earliest market price.

Mid Cap – An altcoin with a medium market capitalization – generally in the hundreds of millions to low billions.

Miner – A computer, under the Proof of Work algorithm, that solves complex equations to create new blocks for unconfirmed transactions.

Moving Averages – A technical indicator displayed as a colored line(s) that averages price action over a select period of time.

Order Book – The unfilled bids and offers listed on an exchange.

Oscillator – A technical tool (portrayed as a line between two values) that travels alongside the general price action of an asset showing some corresponding data or data relationship with the primary price of an asset.

Pennant – A short-term chart pattern formed under 21 days with a pole and consolidation period shaped like a triangle or wedge.

Position Trader – A longer term trader who keeps positions open for weeks, months, or sometimes even years.

Price – The cost of a single asset unit (i.e. one bitcoin is $5,000).

Price Action – The movement of an asset's price over time, which is the foundation of all technical analysis.

Proof of Stake – A popular consensus algorithm used to forge blocks of transactions based on the random or semi-random selection of validator computers ("stakers").

Proof of Work – A popular consensus algorithm used to create and validate blocks of transactions based on the heavy computational power of miner computers.

Pump – A sharp and quick rise in asset value.

Pump and Dump – When an asset's value rises sharply before being sold-off heavily (often used as a form of manipulation and orchestrated by bad actors).

Relative Strength Index (RSI) – A momentum oscillator used to show overbought and oversold conditions, which measures the strength of buying vs. selling over an examined period.

Resistance Line – A trend line in which three or more highs connect showing the higher trend of price action where the buyers are unable to push the price above.

Retest – When an asset's price revisits a previous trend line or other marker of support/resistance.

Retrace – A temporary decline in asset value following an upward move.

Rounding Bottom – A reversal chart pattern marked by a series of lows that trend downward before turning upward creating a bowl-like shape.

Rounding Top – A reversal chart pattern marked by a series of highs that trend upward before turning downward creating an inverted bowl-like shape.

Scalp Trader – A very short-term trader who capitalizes on the smallest market movements and trades very short time frames down to even single minutes.

Sell – To rid yourself of possession of an asset through a sale.

Sell Offer – A seller's posted sale offer of an asset.

Sell Wall – A large sell offer on the order book.

Short – To bet against an asset's price rise with an expectation of profit – often on margin (loaned funds).

Small Cap – An altcoin with a small market capitalization – generally from the thousands to tens of millions.

Spoofing – A widely illegal market manipulation where a trader intentionally puts up fake buy or sell walls to influence the price action of the market.

Squeeze – When the market moves opposite to a market participant such that the participant is forced to close their position and buy or sell; thus, further driving an asset's price up or down.

Stable Coin – A crypto token designed to always maintain a stable value based on a fiat currency (i.e. $1 USD).

Staker – A validator computer that is randomly or semi-randomly chosen and rewarded for forging blocks based on collateral they stake to the network in the blockchain's native currency.

Stop-Limit Order – A two input order telling an exchange a specific price to trigger and execute a limit order.

Stop-Loss – A stop-limit or stop-market order used to close a trade gone bad.

Stop-Market Order – An order telling an exchange a specific price to execute a market order.

Support Line – A trend line in which three or more lows connect showing the lower trend of price action where the sellers are unable to push the price below.

Swing Trader – A trader who keeps a position open for several days to a few weeks.

Symmetrical Triangle – A triangular chart pattern with symmetrical converging support and resistance lines formed over 21+ days.

Technical Analysis – The study of price action used to help predict future market movements.

Time Frame – The select period of time a trader wishes to see price action, which is often displayed in candle form (i.e. 1H, 4H, 1D, 1W).

Token – A crypto issued on a blockchain that is not the native coin (i.e. an ERC-20 Ethereum token but not Ethereum itself).

Trend Channel – When an asset's price ranges between two parallel support and resistance lines.

Trend Line – Three or more highs or lows connected showing the trend of price action.

Triple Bottom – A reversal chart pattern appearing after a downtrend and marked by three distinct lows at or nearly at the same level with two failed rallies in between.

Triple Top – A reversal chart pattern appearing after an uptrend and marked by three distinct highs at or nearly at the same level with two bearish valleys in between.

Volume – The aggregate amount of an asset bought or sold in a period of time (usually described in $ rather than units).

Wallet – The public and private keys used to send and receive a crypto.

Wick – A thin line of a candle representing where the price went before it changed course.

Pattern Performance Analysis Methodology

This project aims to help traders better understand the performance of commonly occurring chart patterns in the volatile cryptocurrency markets. This may be achieved, in part, by examining frequencies of upward and downward breaks; prevalence of continuations and reversals for each pattern; and averaging the % gain or decline following a particular chart pattern's breakout or breakdown. The measurements are designed to help traders anticipate average price action movements between a breakout or breakdown and the next consolidation period or trend reversal of relative size to the examined pattern. Please read the methodology carefully to best understand how to interpret the charts and statistics!

Time Frames

All charts are on the one-day time frame.

Price Action %

Price action % movement is based on the next trend reversal or identifiable major consolidation relative to the examined pattern's size.

Considerations may include the examined pattern's successive pattern/consolidation duration and size, the initial run-up of the examined pattern (i.e. pole length), and any trend break following the initial pattern.

Additionally, if a following period of consolidation is not relatively similar in size to the original pattern, two or more consecutive periods equal to the original pattern duration/size may be counted.

Dashes

Dashes (default blue but green or red on major reversal patterns) represent the close point of the previous trade for the calculation. Some price levels have two dashes if two patterns close at that point (relative to their size).

Breakouts

Breakouts and breakdowns are at trend break - not confirmation.

Color Coding

Continuation pattern trend lines and dashes are blue, while major reversal pattern lines are green or red depending on bottoms or tops, respectively. Some larger patterns may be given a red/green dash or trend line for clarity.

"C" and "R" Distinctions

Each continuation-biased pattern is marked with either C (continuation) or R (reversal). These designate whether the breakout or breakdown is in direct continuation or reversal from the immediate trend behind it (relative to the examined pattern). It does not mean sustained reversal or continuation.

For example, if a flag or pennant is examined, the direction in which the pole stems from.

Trend Lines

Pattern trend lines are created by connecting wicks and bodies, whichever best averages the price action. However, wicks are given first preference.

Gain & Loss %

Price action movement is rounded to the nearest .5%.

Gains are provided under three tiers: 1) unfiltered, 2) outliers over 400% filtered, and 3) gainers over 100% are filtered.

Triangle Duration

Triangles require pattern formation of 21 days or greater (including the day of breakout). Wedge and triangular shapes under 21 days are qualified as pennants.

Falling and Rising Wedges

Whether rising and falling wedges are marked as R or C depends on the immediate preceding trend relative to the size of the wedge. Falling wedges by their very nature arc in a downtrend and when breaking up, they reverse their own trend. However, for the C and R designation, I look to the relative trend intact before the shape began. Thus, even if a falling wedge breaks up, it may be a continuation – despite breaking its own long-lasting downtrend.

Triangle, Wedge, and Pennant Trend Lines

Triangles and wedges require 5+ touches on support and resistance lines. Pennants can be formed by fewer with tight consolidation.

Reversal Necklines

Reversals like double tops/bottoms are preferably played with slanted necklines rather than horizontal necklines depending on chart disposition (obvious diagonal necklines will supersede horizontal ones played at the valley low). As discussed further in the handbook, this is a more aggressive strategy than creating necklines solely from valley lows.

Double tops and bottoms may also include those that are uneven.

Flags

Flags include all square, parallelogram, and rectangular patterns (can be sideways, downward, or upward) over any duration. Flags require 4+ touches on support and resistance lines.

USD Pairs

For USD traded pairs, USD calculated by Tradingview is used over USD or USDT if it allows greater chart history or clearer interpretation.

Pattern Documentation and Exclusions

Not every single identifiable pattern on every chart is documented but the clearest and largest generally are.

Some stable coins and cryptos with insufficient chart history are excluded. For example, FLEXA (insufficient data), HIVE (insufficient data), USDT, PAX, USDC, TUSD, USCD, HYN (no exchange data), and DAI.

References:

[i] Lam, Eric. "Hackers Steal $40 Million Worth of Bitcoin From Binance Exchange." Bloomberg.com, 8 May 2019, www.bloomberg.com/news/articles/2019-05-08/crypto-exchange-giant-binance-reports-a-hack-of-7-000-bitcoin.

[ii] Norry, Andrew. "The History of the Mt Gox Hack: Bitcoin's Biggest Heist." Blockonomi, 31 Mar. 2020, www.blockonomi.com/mt-gox-hack/.

[iii] "5 Biggest Crypto Exchange Hacks of 2019." Bitcoinist.com, 26 Dec. 2019, www.bitcoinist.com/5-biggest-crypto-exchange-hacks-of-2019/.

[iv] Saul, Josh. "New Zealand Crypto Firm Hacked to Death, Seeks U.S. Bankruptcy." Bloomberg.com, www.bloomberg.com/news/articles/2019-05-24/new-zealand-crypto-firm-hacked-to-death-seeks-u-s-bankruptcy.

[v] Pirus, Benjamin. "Tether Claims to Be Okay With Merger of Class-Action Lawsuits Against It." Cointelegraph.com, 17 Jan. 2020, www.cointelegraph.com/news/tether-claims-to-be-okay-with-merger-of-class-action-lawsuits-against-it.

[vi] See e.g., https://www.paxos.com/company/; https://www.circle.com/en/usdc; https://support.usdc.circle.com/hc/en-us/articles/360015478291-How-is-this-regulated-

[vii] https://www.hedera.com/hh-hbar-coin-economics-paper-100919-v2.pdf

[viii] Silkjær, Thomas. "14 Common Misunderstandings About Ripple And XRP." Forbes.com, 7 Mar. 2019, www.forbes.com/sites/thomassilkjaer/2019/03/07/14-common-misunderstandings-about-ripple-and-xrp/#45d4328f71d0.

[ix] "Breaking: A new bull market has begun. The Dow has rallied more than 20% since hitting a low three days ago, ending the shortest bear market ever." Wall Street Journal, Mar. 27 2020, tweet available at: https://twitter.com/WSJ/status/1243267094852055041.

[x] See Bitmex.com on fees. Available at: https://www.bitmex.com/app/fees.

[xi] For more information, see https://www.bitmex.com/app/perpetualContractsGuide.

[xii] See Nison, Steve. Japanese candlestick charting techniques: a contemporary guide to the ancient investment techniques of the Far East. (1991).

[xiii] The Pattern Site. (2005-2019). Bulkowski on the Bullish Three Line Strike, Retrieved June 22, 2020 from http://thepatternsite.com/ThreeLineStrikeBull.html.

[xiv] See e.g., Bulkowski, Thomas N. Trading Classic Chart Patterns. New York, NY: John Wiley & Sons, Inc., 2002.

[xv] The Pattern Site. (2005-2019). Bulkowski's Symmetrical Triangles, Retrieved June 22, 2020 from http://thepatternsite.com/st.html#:~:text=Symmetrical%20Triangles%3A%20Example&text=The%20consolidation%20pattern%20of%20the,to%20a%20strong%20move%20upward; see also Bulkowski, Thomas N. Trading Classic Chart Patterns. New York, NY: John Wiley & Sons, Inc., 2002.

[xvi] Id.

[xvii] See e.g., Bulkowski, Thomas N. Trading Classic Chart Patterns. New York, NY: John Wiley & Sons, Inc., 2002 (noting he found them on thehardrightedge.com).

[xviii] See Wilder, J Welles. New Concepts in Technical Trading Systems. Trend Research, 1978.

Printed in Poland
by Amazon Fulfillment
Poland Sp. z o.o., Wrocław

24801364R00109